NEVER LOSE YOUR
SWAGGER

Intellectualism. Character. Style. Confidence:
Qualities of A King!

Never Lose Your SWAGGER

For more information:

BENTLEY CORPORATE FIRM, INC
FORT LAUDERDALE, FLORIDA 33309
Website: www.BentleyCoachingInstitute.com

Book Cover Illustration & Interior
Website: www.YourCompanyNeedsAWebsite.com

Modified City Image on Cover Provided By:
Flickr.com/photos/paulobar/

ISBN-13: 978-0615627991
ISBN-10: 0615627994

Printed in the United Stated of America

Never Lose Your SWAGGER

TABLE OF CONTENTS

NEVER LOSE YOUR SWAGGER
NEVER LOSE YOUR SWAGGER
NEVER LOSE YOUR SWAGGER
NEVER LOSE YOUR SWAGGER
NEVER LOSE YOUR SWAGGER
NEVER **LOSE** YOUR SWAGGER
NEVER LOSE YOUR SWAGGER
NEVER LOSE YOUR SWAGGER
NEVER LOSE YOUR SWAGGER
NEVER LOSE YOUR SWAGGER
NEVER LOSE **YOUR** SWAGGER
NEVER LOSE YOUR SWAGGER
NEVER LOSE YOUR SWAGGER
NEVER LOSE YOUR SWAGGER
NEVER LOSE YOUR SWAGGER
NEVER LOSE YOUR **SWAGGER**

PROLOGUE

M anhood is changing. It's as simple, and as complicated, as that. Two recent events prompted me to write about swagger and manhood today.

The first was the release of The Shriver Report, a study of the status of women in the United States.

The second was the publication of **The Art of Manliness**, a book of advice on manhood based on the popular blog of the same name. The Shriver Report's most stunning finding is that women now make up half of the American workforce and are the primary breadwinner or co-breadwinner in 2/3 of American families.

While I think the report goes too far in calling us "a woman's nation" – for one thing, women still earn much less, both in terms of average annual income and lifetime income, than men – it does highlight a significant change in American culture.

People my age and under will most likely never know a workplace in which men and women don't figure at least equally. The Art of Manliness is one sign of this change.

While I haven't read the book yet, I've been following the blog since its inception and to boil it down to its essence: Men are not quite sure how to be men anymore.

Masculinity has been constructed over the last century almost entirely around the idea of men as **providers** and **protectors**, and quite frankly, women don't need that any more.

Already in at least a dozen major metropolitan areas, women earn on average more than men. Women are waiting longer to get married, and are more often the initiators of divorce. With their own incomes, they can afford to be pickier about their spouses, both going into marriage and when deciding whether to continue their relationships.

This has all happened in the context of larger social changes that have eliminated a great many jobs that were traditionally the sole province of men – the manufacturing and heavy labor jobs that relied on a powerful physique and a kind of working class swagger, most of which have been either automated or off-shored.

At the same time, a new knowledge economy has sprung up, privileging communication, creativity, and self-motivation over brawn and emotional control.

While there's no inherent reason why women should do better in these emerging businesses than men, the fact is that men have largely given over the field while wasting time twiddling our thumbs over the loss of jobs where "men could be men".

What do I mean? Well, women now make up the majority of college and grad school students, even in many areas in science and technology traditionally considered to be men's domains.

Boys almost never read; only some **1 out of 5** young adult books are read by boys who have determined that reading books is for sissies. Boys are more likely to drop out of high school (35% of boys vs 28% of girls in 2003).

Basically, instead of learning how to be men in a changing world, we've been boys, dragged kicking and screaming into a world where women are increasingly equal players in all aspects of business and life.

Emphasis on "kicking"; instead of figuring out how to do this new thing, we've focused most of our energy on simply emphasizing the characteristics that traditionally defined masculinity, namely toughness and physical brawn. Even our toys have been affected!

Have you ever noticed how action figures have changed? They've become more muscular, conveying a greater impression of raw physical power.

This wouldn't be especially remarkable if not for the fact that physical prowess is less and less needed in our society; even in the military.

These toys embody ideals that are increasingly disconnected with the reality that we live in; a kind of ironic nostalgia for a time when "men were men". (Ironic because, when we look back at those men, they were quite a bit softer and less physically imposing than we think!)

In the end, the exaggerated emphasis on toughness and overall physical strength are misleading and in addition to creating a great deal of violence in our society by those who embrace those ideals, they are preventing us from thinking in constructive ways about the kind of men we could be in today's world.

And that's too bad, because the changes we're living in are largely positive – men are, or could be, much more connected with their families and their partners.

Women are getting the opportunity to develop identities that aren't solely defined by motherhood and the workforce is getting a much larger pool of people to draw talent from.

Around the world, women are emerging as major players in the increasingly global economy. One sign of the role women are playing is the success of the microloan movement, many of whose programs lend primarily or solely to women.

I don't claim that I have all the answers, by the way. I am as prone to chauvinistic thinking, objectification of women, and just plain dumb behavior as the next guy.

It's the way we've been socially and culturally conditioned — creating unconscious thought processes that aren't always immediately apparent. The best I think we can hope for is self-awareness and growth, not the instant transformation of every man into a superhero overnight.

It will be the next generation, the kids who grow up in a world where women are full participants in our public lives, that will show us best how to be men that embrace true equality – and I have no doubt that they'll look on me as unkindly as I look on, say, the anti-Suffragists of the last century.

WE'RE ALL FEMINISTS NOW

Aside from a few hard-core traditionalists, just about everyone now accepts as a given that both men and women will have an education, a career, and a public life.

Each and every one of us benefits daily from the greater participation of women in our society: we use medicines developed by women, we use products designed by women, we live by laws written by and voted on by women, and so on.

By lowering the barriers that prevented women from developing to their fullest extent in the past, we have effectively doubled the pool of talent that we as a society draw on.

The idea that a woman can't be this or that is falsified by the reality that there is virtually no job category that women haven't entered and excelled in.

Real men encourage those around them, male or female, to realize their fullest potential, regardless of their own or others' preconceptions.

That's feminism.

There is no "men's work" and "women's work", there is only work. Sociologists estimate that there are as many as 2 million stay-at-home dads in the US right now.

And fathers as a whole – stay-at-home dads or otherwise – spend almost as much time with their children as mothers do. Men do laundry, cook dinner, buy groceries, and drop the kids off at soccer practice.

Meanwhile, women write legal briefs, run for office, work construction equipment, and direct corporate mergers. The idea that certain kinds of work are "feminine" or "masculine" is dead in the water.

Although there are plenty of holdouts who are still inclined to fill positions based at least in part on gender, the most successful businesses work hard to focus their hiring on demonstrated talent.

Likewise, the most successful families split household tasks not according to gender but according to skill and available time.

There are plenty of un-handy men around, and plenty of non-domestic women, and we all benefit when they're encouraged to do the things they're good at instead of the things their gender allegedly suits them for.

PARENTING IS FUNDAMENTAL

The reason that so many men are choosing to spend all or a significant part of their lives elbow-deep in domestic parenting tasks is that we are finally learning how much we've been missing in our traditional 8am-8pm work+commute+overtime workaholic schedules.

Whole generations of men have missed not only seeing their kids grow up, but seeing themselves grow up. Parenting is about so much more than financially supporting someone through their childhood years, it's about tending to cuts and scrapes, putting a balanced meal on the table and dealing with the scores of childhood traumas that mark our growth into adulthood.

It's about sacrifice, hands-on responsibility, and struggling alongside our kids to make sense of the world. The stereotypical middle-aged man sporting a ponytail and a convertible is, I think, a product of the kind of selfishness that real parenting eliminates.

Never Lose Your SWAGGER

PASSION IS A PRIORITY

Manhood in the 20th century was about financial success. It was about working a job you hate simply because it puts food on the table. With both men and women supporting their families, though, some of that pressure is lifted. Of course, we still need to work, but just as important as earning a living is the passion that drives us to excel – even at careers that are not especially lucrative.

We can see, for instance, the rise of "lifestyle entrepreneurs". These are people who start their own businesses not so much in hopes of getting rich but in order to support themselves doing something they love, as an indicator of the way that income is giving way to passion as a measure of one's manhood.

EMBRACE DIFFERENCE

It's becoming harder and harder to take people who rant about the difference between men and women seriously.

For every generalization, we can point to a thousand exceptions – men who love shopping and women who hate it, women who whoop and holler over their football team's victory and men who couldn't tell you if the Cleveland Browns play in the American League or the National League.

Traditional masculinity was about punishing any man who stepped out of bounds, whether it was because he was gay, feminine, physically weak, or in some other way short of the masculine standard.

That simply doesn't fly any more – there are as many different ways of being "manly" (or "womanly", for that matter) as there are men (or women). And success doesn't come in spite of those differences, it comes because of it. Those differences create the diversity that allows businesses, organizations, and other endeavors to be flexible, to adapt to changing circumstances, and to innovate.

In short, difference allows us to thrive and we need to stop fearing it and embrace it.

And that goes for other kinds of differences, too – racial, ethnic, sexual orientation, religious, national, linguistic, you name it. Being a confident man these days means not being threatened by what we don't understand, it means seeking greater understanding.

IT's ABOUT US

Though "being one's own man" has long been held up as a standard of masculinity, it's rarely been realized in practice.

The eras of manhood that we look back to nostalgically as models of "when men were men" – I'm thinking, for example, of the Mad Men era – were times of stunning conformity.

We weren't our own men, we were beholden to a particularly narrow model of what men should be, and men who didn't fit that model were punished, often brutally.

The 21st century offers men a real opportunity to live up to the ideal of being our own men, though. The possibilities for personal development and self-expression have never been greater.

It's no longer about what women find attractive – freed from the need to find man to support and protect them, women are finding themselves attracted to a wide range of types that in the past might have been considered "unmanly".

It's no longer about being "one of the boys" – that kind of conformity is poison to the modern workplace and to modern communities.

No, manhood today is about us, about living our own lives as fully and satisfyingly as we can.

IT's ABOUT YOU

Like I said, I don't have all the answers, and I'm intensely curious about your thoughts. I've left some things out, too – most notably sex, but also fashion, personality, and matters of taste or style.

These things have become so expansive that there's no way I could do them any justice here.

By and large, I think they fall under the category of embracing difference – of recognizing that in a society where diversity is a crucial value, men will find a huge variety of ways to dress, act, enjoy their leisure time, and make love.

FOREWORD

M en are the architects of nations and our nations are in crisis. As a man succeeds or fails, so does his family, the society and the world he lives in.

The concern at hand is that men have lost their identity and don't have a precise direction for their lives thus the consequences for their families, communities, and nations are a major concern.

DIVERGENCE OF MANHOOD

The role of the male continues to exist from one generation to another. Today men are confused about who they are and what functions they play in the agenda of life. The standard customary pursuits in life such as working, marrying, and having a family are the usual standards for men.

There is also a level of uncertainty and low **SELF-ESTEEM** that exist among men.

Society plays an essential role in the development of men and often times the standard by which men are measured **IS** inaccurate sending out conflicting signals about what it means to be a man. The world is rapidly evolving before us, and the social alterations accompanying it can be a painful experience.

The clash of the old and new meanings regarding men has left many men perplexed and frustrated as it relates to their masculinity and identity.

Men attempt to make the necessary adjustments and adapt to social expectations that are apparent in life. Amidst all of the changes, there is a desire to maintain and hold on to his personal **Swagger**.

A REDISCOVERY OF YOUR SWAGGER

"Give a man power and you will reveal his true character." ~ *Lincoln*

I think the quote *"Give a man power and you will reveal his true character"* means that if you give a man the right to speak out and stand up for his rights you will see the power in him.

I think it means that when a man is given the freedom he needs, he has this person inside of him that's ready to stand up and show it off to everybody.

A man without power is a man in search of it.

If you are looking for a book to show you how to reclaim your personal power and get swagger, you've found the right book! To have swagger means that you have high self-confidence and you're outgoing.

You can spot someone with swagger from a mile away. It makes sense that you want to know how to get swagger and reading this book is the first step…

I'm going to discuss the physiology (physical aspect), as well as the psychology (mental aspect) of how to get swagger.

The physiology (physical aspect) of a person with swagger:

- **Alpha Posture:** When you see someone who has swagger they definitely have amazing posture. It's almost impossible to be seen as having swagger if you're slouched over. Good posture is a sign of high self-confidence.

   Not only do you look more alpha when your posture is proper but you also feel more confident within. Your physiology is one of the keys to the way you feel.

   If you stand and walk like a person who has swagger you will be perceived as a person who has swagger and like it or not, perception is reality.

- **Alpha Body Language:** A study by UCLA showed as much as 93 percent of communication effectiveness is in your body language. Ninety-three percent! That shows you how important it is to master the art of body language. Body language is literally the language of the body.

- **Smile:** Learn to manipulate and use the muscles in your face. A smile speaks a thousand words. People are drawn towards others who make them feel good and important. I can't think of any better way to make others feel good in an instant than a smile. People with swagger make other people feel good so SMILE!

Now that we've covered the physical aspect of how to get swagger let's move on to the mental aspect.

The psychology (mental aspect) of having swagger:

- **Self-Confidence:** One of the main traits a person with swagger possesses is self-confidence. In order for people to think you have swagger they must think you have self-confidence. I'd go as far as to say that you can define swagger as self-confidence!

Never Lose Your SWAGGER

- **Indifference To What Others Think:** A core belief that I always stress is not caring what anyone thinks of you. This belief works wonders for you on the inside but also reflects on the outside and shows that you're self-assured and have a positive self-image.

  If you make this belief a part of you, you're well on your way to having swagger. And remember, it doesn't matter what people call you, it only matters what you answer to.

- **Knowing You Have Swagger:** The key to having swagger is in knowing that you have swagger! If you believe on the inside that you have swagger it will reflect on the outside. No one can have swagger unless they have a deep belief on the inside that they have swagger! Start today to truly believe that you have swagger!

You now have a decent idea of some of the mental keys to having swagger. The educational (intellectual aspect) of having swagger:

- **Intellect:** Intellectualism is a distinguished character trait.

- **Can Entertain Himself:** The educated man is insatiably curious about the world around him and other people. In any situation, he sees something to learn, study, and observe.

  If he's stuck on something, he uses the time to untangle a philosophical problem he's been wrestling with. The mind of the educated man is a repository of ideas that he can pull out and examine to pass the time in any situation.

- **Can Entertain Friends:** The educated man is the life of the party; the man who keeps the conversation lively and is known to be unfailingly engaging.

He is able to do this because of the breadth of his reading and his experiences. He has an arsenal of interesting tales at the ready about his travels and endeavors. And he's up on the latest news stories and interesting scientific breakthroughs.

No matter the demographics of the group he's with, he knows a story that will appeal to them.

- **<u>Can Entertain A New Idea:</u>** Rather, you should entertain an idea in the same way you entertain a guest. You talk with him in a public setting first, at a distance. If you're intrigued, you then invite him over for a chat.

    You spend some time getting to know him. And if he turns out to be a bad apple, you stop letting him come around. But sometimes, the person you didn't think you had anything in common with becomes your new best friend.

    The educated man has an easier time in seeing this. His varied experiences and studies have given him multiple opportunities to see how the information he has learned has changed his opinions, even if it took those new ideas a long time to be invited in.

    The sheltered man who only interacts with people just like him and only reads things that confirm his preconceived ideas will not have these experiences to draw upon, and will thus greet all new ideas like menacing strangers, shaking his fist at them from the safety of the other side of his crocodile-infested moat.

    Have you heard about "swagger"? It's the new thing to have and if you don't have it and self-confidence then you are on the outside looking in.

    If you desire to be part of "it" then you are going to need to follow these steps on how to have swagger today!

THE AUTHENTIC ME

When I realized my greatest potentials, gifts, and talents; I made a conscientious decision to pursue my purpose without fail and to contribute to humanity in tremendous ways. I have found the "Authentic Me".

I didn't fit the (mold) of many and I don't intend too. From this point: it's on and popping.

- J'Ramando Horton

Never Lose Your SWAGGER

SWAGGER INSTRUCTIONS

Walk proud and have self-confidence. The first step in having self-confidence is being your own personal cheerleader.

Be a leader and not a follower. This is the trademark of how to have your own swagger. The way you talk and the way you walk are all you, so own it. There is only one of you in this whole wide world, so be proud of everything about you.

CHECK THIS SWAGGER OUT

Have style and respect.

Represent your own personal style and be confident in your style. People who demand respect when they walk in a room all have their own individual swagger.

Stop following the crowd and don't think that anyone has anything on your moves. Building confidence and self-esteem is a must if you want people to respect you.

Your demeanor is the key to your success; if you are confident in yourself others will be confident in you also. Most people will follow someone who is leading the way so be that leader.

YEAH BABY, THIS IS CONFIDENCE

Be self-reliant and rely on yourself for anything you need. Don't expect anything from others and you will never be disappointed. Have confidence in anything you are doing. If you are doing it then it must be the new cool thing to do, right?

If you have swagger the answer here would always be "yes".

HAVE SWAGGER TODAY

Realize that swagger is the self-worth and self-confidence that you have for yourself. Set a high standard for yourself and live up to it. You determine the manner in which you represent who you are from the moment you walk in a room, so represent you at your best!

Some men are born with it; some acquire it after hanging out with a certain crowd or attending a certain school. Either way it goes, women are always attracted to men with swagger. . .

You know, when a girl says "There's just something about him, I can't really describe it. . ." that's swagger.

To be real, there are many of you that may not need it as much because you may have strong traits that make up for it: good looks w/ a smile to match, great abs and muscles, or big pockets.

But, even men with those traits find themselves in dire need of swagger. Many guys falsely believe that swagger only comes with hard jail time, being a dealer, or being in a gang.

That's just called ignorance, which usually leads to arrogance and perhaps a forced swagger.

There's nothing cool about killing someone. . .

True swagger, as corny as it sounds, comes from within and that makes it hard to gain. Swagger can be traditionally characterized as charisma; that indescribable character trait that people naturally inhibit. Swagger is like charisma to the umpteenth power with a mixture of more.

It doesn't discriminate by age, race, height, or background. Anyone can have it.

There are 3 main components to swagger:

- **Confidence:** - Being comfortable with who you are is very important. If you don't think you're the ish, then why should anyone else? There are many ways to gain confidence, but a couple of the fastest ways are:

  1. **Working Out**: Bulking up easily boosts your self-confidence and makes a woman do a double-take.

2. **New Wardrobe:** Many men underestimate the importance of dressing well. They think it's a female thing. But great threads will make you feel better and quickly enhance your image in the eyes of others.

- **Drive/Direction:** I'm not referring to sex .I'm talking about ambition. Men with the most swagger know what they want in life. They have goals and they don't let anyone get in their way. If you have problems focusing, try this:

1. Write down your top 5 career choices and the steps you need to take to actually become whatever it is you want to become. Try and narrow it down to the most realistic career choice available to you and go after it.

2. Make a list of goals you have and set a deadline to have each goal completed.

3. **Be You.** Like the rapper Rocko says "You just do you and I'll do me". At the end of the day it's all about doing you. Be who you are and no apologies unless you're being a complete jerk.

Now that you know what swagger is and how to get it- work on it! **Every urban gentleman must find his inner swag.**

Perfecting your swagger could be the most important thing you do as a single person. Swagger is more than a pimped out strut, it's a mystical energy exuded by a man or a woman that tells the world they're confident and ready for anything or anybody.

Ladies, you've seen it before, a man walks into a bar and you can't help but wonder what it is about him that seems to draw you to him.

Men, it's the same thing when you see a woman walk into a bar or club and she's got a quiet confidence that drives you wild the minute you lay eyes on her.

While swagger comes naturally for some, if you can learn to master it, you will definitely get the edge in the singles scene.

Never Lose Your SWAGGER

Gentlemen, if you have no idea what swagger is, go rent every Denzel Washington movie there is. This is swagger. While you may not have the skills to get to Denzel's level, I'm sure you can grab a few pointers from him. In any situation where you're unsure of what to do, ask yourself "WWDD" (what would Denzel do)?

Ladies, if you have no idea what female swagger is, look in the mirror. It is you, it is acceptance. It is confidence in your essence, who you are inside and out.

Ladies cannot "swagger jack" like men and mimic someone else's swagger, because it will come across as phony. Really love who you are and your swagger will flow naturally.

A GENTLEMAN WITH SWAGGER

A gentleman is polite, decent and known for his courteous conduct.

He is a man of principles. To look at the characteristics of a gentleman, read on…

Today, we use the word 'gentleman' very casually, without understanding the depth in its meaning.

Any audience, large or small, is addressed by the terms ladies and gentlemen.

On looking at the real deep meaning of the word 'gentleman' we realize how carelessly we use it. The word 'gentleman' has evolved over a long time.

The word is associated with esteemed values and principles that should be possessed by a man to be called a gentleman. The connotation of the word 'gentleman' has changed over time.

It once implied a man of **conduct**, a man of **virtue** while it has become an everyday word of the present which is truly a shame.

CHARACTERISTICS OF A GENTLEMAN WITH A SWAGGER

Being a gentleman does not depend on the social standing of a man. It is his **behavior**, which makes him a gentleman. According to an old story, a woman had requested the king to make her son a gentleman.

The king had replied to her saying that he would only be able to make him a nobleman and only God would be able to make him a gentleman. During the Shakespearean Era, a man who bore a coat of arms was considered a gentleman.

During the olden days, wearing a sword was one of the visible characteristics of gentlemen.

A gentleman was supposed to hold good moral values and be loyal and pious. A man who sought justice and always stood by humaneness was considered a gentleman among other gentlemen.

With the passing time, the word 'gentleman' began to be linked to a wider range of characteristics.

Today, one may associate a gentleman with gentleness. But the real significance of the word was a man's characteristic of gentility. A gentleman is one who treats others, especially women with respect. It is he who bears great regard towards womanhood.

It is he who understands her and treats her honorably. A gentleman is characterized by his courtesy and concern towards women. He gives ladies their due respect and acts with humility.

It's the decency in a man's behavior that characterizes him as a gentleman and a man of superior qualities; **An Alpha Man**.

A gentleman is someone who does not take an undue advantage of his power or the weaknesses of those around him. He is a man who does not compel others to do anything against their wishes. A gentleman never offends others physically or mentally.

He never inflicts pain. In a broader sense of the term, a gentleman is the one who cares for the people around him, helps them with their problems and strives to remove every obstacle that impedes their lives. Easing and comforting everyone around remains the major concern of a gentleman.

He is a thoughtful and has foresight. His wisdom helps him stay away from blunders.

Other characteristics of a gentleman include his humbleness, his prudence, his calm, his patience and his principles. A gentleman never boasts of himself.

He is merciful and tender. He can keep his cool in all types of situations. He never looks at people with prejudiced eyes. He refrains from getting into conflicts or debates. He keeps himself away from badmouthing people and making unreasonable allegations.

He strongly dislikes gossip.

Above all, a gentleman bases his thoughts and actions on healthy philosophical principles. He submits to pain and understands that certain things in life are inevitable. He accepts death as a part of destiny. He adheres to righteousness throughout life.

Now think for yourself, how many 'gentlemen' do you know?

QUINTESSENTIAL BEAST

What makes a man a Quintessential Beast?

What qualities and talents must one have to exude the strong, masculine, intelligent, sexy, appeal of the Alpha Male?

Many, but most importantly the following Eight Principles:

A QUINTESSENTIAL BEAST IS RESPONSIBLE

We were once a gender of Beasts; men that stood higher and mightier than their circumstances, individuals who understood the meaning and opportunity in fear and the fact little can come without risk.

We were **husbands of integrity, fathers of example** and **leaders of conviction**. And I fear that this could all be lost and by our own doing.

We are all responsible for the condition that surrounds us, on a personal level and on a universal level. Day after day I stand in awe, observant of man's ability to rise above physical inferiority, mental limitations, and social blocks to create for him a unique chapter in the books of our doing.

Likewise I am amazed by all those things we have killed, deteriorated, depleted and corrupted.

All by our doing.

I wonder what our forefathers would think of email or texting as it quickly replaces essential daily human interaction. What would they say of processed food or childhood obesity? How they would laugh at our dating sites. And what would they think of divisive political strategy or the fact that men no longer open doors or pull out chairs?

I refuse to be a part of a generation that is associated with societal breakdown, environmental corruption, economic perdition and unfocused wars.

For this reason, Modern Beast brings you the world that surrounds us through an angle of **responsibility**, **brutal honesty**, and **intelligence**, written for the man responsible for all that surrounds him, creator of his failures and *master craftsman* of his success.

A QUINTESSENTIAL BEAST DISPLAYS STRENGTH

Strength is far more than muscle on wrench. We speak of *strength of conviction* and pursuit. Know your strengths, understand your weaknesses. In a resourceful world it is hard not to defer a situation to the aid or handling of others. Not for a beast, a man of strength creates solutions, one way or another.

It is in our moments of peril that we find the extent of our moral, physical and social capacities.

It is the application of such capacities that dictate the extent of our strength.

A QUINTESSENTIAL BEAST HONORS DUTY

Society has issued man a debilitating curve ball. Apparently, duty has been supplanted by comfort and "feelings" in exchange of good old fashion responsibilities.

We are men associated to fatherless children and single mothers. We divorce women as often as we change cars. This is not a matter of male/female relations, this matter of duty. Choose wisely and stick with that choice.

Rid yourself of back doors and escape hatches.

We have learned that jumping from job to job offers the quickest reward, the quickest promotion or raise, leaving behind companies fully staffed with not a single stakeholder to entrust its future with.

We drop out of school because it is not convenient to our leisure, forgetting that our intelligence as men, and yours as a man, is not something to take for granted.

A QUINTESSENTIAL BEAST IS KNOWLEDGEABLE

An education reaches far deeper than degrees and diplomas. A modern beast educates himself in any way necessary, not for the sake of facts and memory, but for the thirst to expand his own horizons.

Raise your hand if you've met an idiot with a PhD. Now raise your hand if you've met a genius without a high school diploma.

Education and the pursuit thereof is a biological necessity. We are an evolving species that needs the constant expansion of our knowledge base.

Television and radio are **not** substitutes for books and courses. How is it that we complain of our failures and do not read which enriches our arsenal with the failure and experience of others? We leave behind vast isles of books gather dust as we cut the links of generational improvement and intellectual expansion?

Never Lose Your SWAGGER

You will never have a unique problem.

No matter what is going on in your life, someone somewhere has written a book with a possible solution in it. You needlessly suffer through situations others have already overcome and written down step-by-step instructions to overcoming if you don't have a thirst for knowledge and a desire to know more.

Knowledge against struggle is like a hammer against a nail. Something has to give and more often than not, it's the nail. Arm yourself with tools for success by expanding your knowledge.

A QUINTESSENTIAL BEAST IS COMMITTED

Be your word men; be your word. What a world we would live in if people did what they said they would do, at the time they said they would do it, in the manner they promised it. We look into our company's eyes and feign professional commitment.

We take the livelihoods and lives of the women that love us as we proclaim empty promises.

A Quintessential Beast is not required to stay at a dead end job or despise a dead relationship out of sheer commitment, he is required that he honor his word; first to himself, and then to the world.

A QUINTESSENTIAL BEAST IS A LEADER

The Quintessential Beast breathes leadership. They need neither a wing-man nor a nudge to step forward.

They believe in giving and charity because not everyone is as blessed as we are and because we believe everyone should be. They always make the first move and always fight at the front line.

A Beast will lead his sons and daughters with as much research, preparation and charisma as he will lead a boardroom. He will lead quietly and by example, always by example, because to lead in any other way is baseless.

For those who have attained success by leading only in proclamation, it is a matter of time, your time ticks, it will fall apart.

They are the first to give credit for the great news and they are the first to deliver and assume responsibility for bad ones. A Quintessential Beast will face his fears, those of his family, those of his staff, and those of his community, boldly, valiantly.

Does this mean they are void of fear? No. They simply act on it. Leadership to a Beast is standing at the forefront of it all, proactively handling business.

Alpha males.

The men that get the girl and save the department. The type of men whose daughters grow up to compare every man they meet to.

Why? Because life will deal difficulties and trepidations anyway, be the first to face them, it will rid yourself of much anxiety and will prompt those around you to understand that moments of trial are prime opportunities to grow.

A QUINTESSENTIAL BEAST IS A LOVER

I see you grinning. That's OK. But a man is only a man if he knows how, who, and when to love. Women, you will notice, are cherished beings to the Quintessential Beast, namely because most of us tend to date and marry 10s, also because good women are embarrassingly more understanding, intelligent, compassionate, wise, and gorgeous than men, including Modern Beasts.

With the women you love, it is not a matter of looks and it is not a matter of money.

Believe this, it is a matter of heart.

And in the matters of love, a Beast always thrives. How? Much like a Beast is a walking success in the corporate world, he is a walking success with the woman that lies beside him. Because he provides a greater attention, care, foresight, detail and work ethic to his women than he does to his money.

We have said this before: A Quintessential Beast loves women one at a time. It is impossible to devote ones full attention to more than one.

Never Lose Your SWAGGER

If you contest this, I guarantee you the women who share your affection will soon find out that they have been getting less than everything of what you have to offer; your time ticks and you will fail.

A Quintessential Man is a lover as a son, as a brother, as a colleague, and as a father. He cherishes the progression of life. He realizes that it is essential to value your childhood, positive or otherwise, because it molded him and it will serve as a platform for him to be the father he had or the father he wished he did.

A QUINTESSENTIAL BEAST IS A MAN

Man.

The epic word... the "In the beginning" type of Man. You know exactly what this means.

It means **be the person they hired, the person she married or fell in love with, the friend and colleague you are expected to be, the person that you truly are but have never managed to be**; a Modern Beast.

Man Up.

DR. J' RAMANDO'S CONJECTURE ON SWAGGER

Swagger is a combination of motivation and self-belief, resulting in a state of mind where you **truly believe** you can achieve anything you put your mind to.

When you have swagger, you have an innate confidence to go after your goals - and you usually achieve them. You are energetic, focused, highly confident and you expect things to go your way.

You feel like you're on top of the world, and almost forget any time in your life when you've felt anything but amazing.

The trouble is, self-belief and focus tends to come and go in waves. One day you're feeling awesome and on top of the world, while the next you feel lazy, lethargic and utterly unmotivated.

Never Lose Your SWAGGER

The aim of this book on motivation and self-belief is to give you practical tips on how to get your swagger back and keep it for longer and longer periods.

Swagger is simply an emotional state and can be replicated. If you've been really confident even once, no matter how long ago, you can get it back now.

WHY IS SWAGGER A GOOD THING?

Before we move on to some strategies for getting your swagger back, I'd like to go into a little more detail about the benefits.

First, being in a state of flow gives you an almost **unshakable self-confidence**. You believe in yourself and expect other people to believe in you too. You hold your head high when you walk and project a feeling of belief and competence to everyone around you.

When things go wrong as they inevitably do, your swagger stops you from getting anxious and worried.

It instead allows you to think effectively and choose the right way to proceed. It's like having a bullet-proof vest for your emotional state. You just don't let things get to you anymore.

ISN'T SWAGGER THE SAME THING AS ARROGANCE?

Nope. Arrogance is an "attitude of superiority" - while swagger is simply an inherent self-belief, coupled with the motivation to go and get what you want.

Arrogance, for many reasons, is seen as a negative trait. Nobody likes an arrogant know-it-all and arrogance, more often than not, is merely a defense shield against deep rooted insecurities.

Arrogance is the opposite of swagger. Swagger is just a feeling of confidence expressed overtly. There is no feeling "superior" to anyone else; you just believe in yourself and go after what you want in life.

This is a positive trait to possess.

Arrogant folk don't tend to get very far. They upset too many people on the road to success. People with swagger on the other hand, people who truly believe in themselves, people who carry themselves like they are already the success they want to be, people who pick themselves up and dust themselves off after setbacks are cool people and have poise.

FEEL AMAZING *NOW!*

I'll share with you with this little technique - I call it "Instant Swagger".

It can help you to generate the physiology and emotional state of belief on demand.

It's just a short term fix and the feelings are not permanent, unfortunately, but it's a great way to cheat if you need to feel confident right now!

It only takes a couple of minutes and after reading through the instructions, you should attempt it right now with your eyes closed.

1. Take a minute now to remember a time when you felt so confident, so assured of success that you felt on top of the world and propelled yourself into taking on whatever challenge was in front of you.

   Find a specific memory. It might have been a big deal you knew you were going to close, somebody you were going to ask on a date, or a presentation you had to give. All that matters is that you had that indescribable feeling that everything was going to go your way...

2. Go back to that great memory now... See what you saw, feel what you felt and put yourself right back in the middle of that phenomenal time in your life. Shut your eyes for a minute or two and really immerse yourself in this great feeling of self-belief and confidence.

3. See the memory through your own eyes. Look around and get a real sense that you are back there now. Let the empowering positive emotions wash over you. Notice what you are feeling and thinking that makes you feel so good.

   Notice your posture and breathing and just enjoy how confident you feel.

4. Make the picture in your mind more vivid, brighter and bigger. Now, double the brightness. Double it again! As you make the picture brighter, double the size of it and then double the emotions you can feel! Now, double them all again!

5. Really ramp up the emotions and try to pick up on every little detail of how you feel. Make the sounds louder, closer and bigger and truly immerse yourself in the vibrancy of the memory.

6. Finally, notice where the feeling of swagger is strongest in your body. Give this feeling of confidence a color and move that color up to the top of your head and then down to your toes. Double the brightness and go up and down your body again...

   Do it again and again until you feel awesome!

   Now... come back to the present... Tell me that didn't feel good?! You've just borrowed a technique from NLP to make a past memory even better than it was the first time... and in doing so, proved that you can access this fantastic state on demand. This is big news - it's basically a cheat to feeling good whenever you like!

Never Lose Your SWAGGER

PERSONAL DEVELOPMENT PLANET ARTICLES ON SELF-BELIEF AND MOTIVATION

It's worth noting that motivation and confidence tend to be cyclical, particularly if in the past you've had a bit of self-doubt. Don't fight this cycle, as I believe that the down periods are essential for rest and growth, but these articles will show you how to feel more confident and motivated when you choose to be.

Having swagger is very much like living in a state of flow - or being "in the zone" - things come to you easier, you genuinely enjoy what you do, and you build an unstoppable momentum that takes you tumbling towards your goals.

Get your Swagger back and enjoy life to the fullest.

THE AUTHENTIC SWAGGER

Adapted from Classy Men

What is the true definition of swagger? Many people are curious for the answer.

Unfortunately for most who search for the it, they often find a "definition" of swagger that is false, contradicting and misleading to the true meaning.

FIRST LET'S DISPEL THE FALSE DEFINITION OF SWAGGER

Ironically enough, these so called "definitions" of swagger, are the EXACT OPPOSITE of what TRUE SWAGGER is.

- To walk or conduct oneself with an insolent or arrogant air. **FALSE**

- To be a bragger or boastful person. **FALSE**

- To conduct oneself in an arrogant or pompous manner. **FALSE**

- To walk with an air of overbearing self-confidence. **FALSE**

These are NOT the definition of swagger, but the definition of a LAME.

THE MAN OF SWAGGER IS THE COMPLETE OPPOSITE OF THESE THINGS

The main reason for this is that someone with TRUE swagger does not need to announce to the entire room that he has swagger.

The people around him just KNOW it, because of his aura and by the way he carries himself.

An arrogant man thinks and acts as if he is superior to others, in turn, causing others to think badly of him and dislike him.

But instead, a man with authentic swagger looks to make others around him feel good. This makes him a desirable person in every way.

People WANT to be in his presence, because he is **fun**, **charismatic**, **pleasant** and **curiously different**.

He has an element of mystery as well, which is intriguing. His charisma is thoroughly enforced because he is well groomed, stylish, suave and a successful communicator. He is the definition of swagger.

To top it all off, all the traits that he possess are **NOT A BIG DEAL** to him at all, but these same traits would be broadcast through a bull horn by an arrogant man, to the dismay and disdain of many.

FINALLY, THE TRUE DEFINITION OF SWAGGER

1. How one presents himself to the world, the ability to handle a situation with a sense of calm and uncanny grace.

   The ability to maintain a healthy level of self-confidence without appearing arrogant.

2. The seeming effortlessness to a person's admired style, the way they walk, talk and dress.

3. The inability to be easily shaken by anyone or anything.

"When you do the common things in life in an uncommon way, you will command the attention of the world."

- George Washington Carver

THE FUNDAMENTALS OF TRUE SWAGGER

Now that you have found the true definition of swagger, we can proceed with some of the finer details. Please understand that very few people are born with swagger, and not everyone that tries to learn and use it succeeds.

But MOST can find some level of success with it.

Even those whose very nature goes contrary to swagger can use certain elements of a person who embodies swagger. It is not necessary to become the very definition of swagger, but adding a little panache to your personality can only help you in the long run.

If you do become the very definition of swagger itself, you probably had a lot inside of you all along, but just didn't know how to fully embrace it yet.

Either way, here are the traits of someone with swagger:

Smiles Often: The smile is highly underrated by many men. A man with true swagger uses his smile as a billboard to advertise his confidence. A genuine smile puts others at ease. A smile denotes happiness and happiness denotes success, because all anybody really wants is happiness anyway. Women are magnetically drawn to a man with a limitless supply of smiles.

Praises Others: Self-confidence is truly shown when a man is comfortable, verbally bringing to attention the good things about others. When appropriate, compliment others liberally. But only if it's sincere, false compliments are easily seen through. People love to talk about themselves and they will love to be around you. THAT is the definition of swagger.

Shows Respect To All: Nothing goes more contrary to the definition of swagger than a disrespectful person. A man of swagger, treats everyone with respect. He does not talk down to those serving or working for him, such as employees, waiters/waitresses, bartenders, etc. A man with swagger also tips appropriately and avoids behaving like a cheap-skate.

Has No Time To Hate: A man of swagger is above talking bad about others for sport. Dwelling on others faults for the sake of conversation is petty and lame to him. He's smart enough to realize that if those around him like to smile in a person's face and then stab that person in the back that his back could just as easily become a landing place for those same knives.

Doesn't Argue With Fools: This is key to maintaining any swagger you may possess. An intelligent debate with another person makes for good conversation and stimulates the brain. BUT, arguing with a fool, even if you are 100% correct, makes you look like a fool as well.

People looking on will not be able to tell the difference. A fool is a person who is overly loud, vulgar, substitutes intellect and communication skills with profanity. From such a person, a man with swagger will take his leave immediately and with no regrets.

Isn't Shy About Leaving: In social situations a man with swagger will often "work the room". That being the case, when a man of swagger needs to move on, he simply moves on. He may have a good reason (as stated above), he may have something or someone else to tend to, or he might just be bored with a conversation.

Whatever the case, he politely excuses himself and leaves. Whether he explains the reason or not is up to him. A man of swagger owns his "presence" and uses it as he sees fit, not allowing himself to become "stuck" anywhere. Besides that, he also realizes that absence makes the heart grow fonder; he will be welcomed back when he returns.

Is Unflappable: A man of swagger is able to "slow the moment" in his head, whatever the case may be. This means that no matter the situation that arises, he keeps his head about him. He is never panicked. He is able to take control of a situation, when it is needed.

Never Lose Your SWAGGER

He is able to follow the lead of someone capable of leading, if it is needed. He doesn't let the emotions of others escalate his emotions. He remains steady and he does not cry over spilled milk.

Understands That Silence Is Deafening: A man of swagger realizes two important truths; these two truths are as follows... First, many people love to bathe in their own ignorance and would love to pull you in with them. Second, that silence is one of the hardest arguments to refute. Being that his swagger attracts people and attention, there will come jealous ones who aim to make him look foolish.

They will throw "swagger daggers" at him. These are insults and mean-spirited jokes with the intent of coaxing an "un-swaggerlike" reaction from him.

The man of swagger reads the situation and remains completely unaffected by these people, he simply converses and laughs "around" these people, in effect, putting them in a "sound booth." His silence towards the hater speaks volumes to everyone observing. The more the hater says about him after this point, makes them look obsessed with him. Soon others will be telling the offender to be quiet or go away.

Masterful.

Can Take Rejection In Stride: A man of swagger realizes that NO MAN WALKING THIS EARTH is immune to rejection so he keeps his ego in check and moves on from rejection with grace.

By the time the rejecter realizes their mistake, the man of swagger is too busy being accepted by someone or something else to be concerned. That is the definition of swagger if ever there were one.

Is Well-Groomed: The man of swagger always maintains top-notch grooming habits. In social and business situations he is NEVER smelly, sloppy, unwashed or unkempt.

(Smelly includes the over-use of bad colognes.) He dresses well and understands what is stylish and what is not. He is ever aware that in order to be the definition of swagger he absolutely MUST be well groomed.

Gives Others Space: Literally and figuratively. Nothing is more annoying than being over-crowded by someone else. Annoying is contrary to the definition of swagger. A close talker CANNOT be a man of swagger, because he makes others feel uncomfortable.

A man of swagger gives people room, he does not warm a person's face with his breath, no matter how pleasant his breath is. No one should be within accidental spittle range!

Secondly, a man of swagger picks up on the signs of other people, if he notices that they seem to be distracted or would like to move on. A man of swagger will give the person an "OUT" or simply move on himself. By doing this, he does the other person and himself a favor.

Talks About What He Knows: A man of swagger does not pretend to know something that he doesn't. He understands that to be a great conversationalist, he should ONLY expound on what he does know and that he should ask questions about what he doesn't know.

In doing this he avoids being found to be a fraud, which is contrary to the definition of swagger. He also understands that if he listens instead of pretending to know something, next time he WILL KNOW enough to expound on the subject without risking his swagger.

CONFIDENCE: YEAH BABY

There are lots of ways to improve your self-confidence over the long-term, but sometimes you need an instant boost.

There are lots of ways to improve your self-confidence over the long-term – but sometimes you need an instant boost.

You can't walk into an important work meeting, (or a class at college or a room full of strangers at a party) whilst frantically re-reading a self-help manual, or making a last-minute phone call to your life-coach.

So here are ten secrets to boosting your self-confidence in just a few seconds...

Never Lose Your SWAGGER

10 Secrets For A Swagger – Confidence

1. **Smile:** The one-second tip for when you're feeling nervous and unconfident is simply to smile! You don't just smile because you are happy and confident – you can smile to make yourself feel better. The act of smiling is so strongly associated with positive feelings that it's almost impossible to feel bad while smiling.

   Smiling is much more than just a facial expression. The simple act of smiling releases feel-good endorphins, improves circulation to the face, makes you feel good about yourself in general and can definitely increase your self-confidence.

   You will also appear more confident to others while you're smiling.

2. **Make Eye Contact:** As well as smiling, meet the eyes of other people in the room. Give them your smile; you'll almost certainly get one back, and being smiled at is a great self-confidence boost.

   Like smiling, eye contact shows people that you're confident. Staring at your shoes or at the table reinforces your feelings of self-doubt and shyness.

   This tip is particularly useful for work-related situations – make eye contact with interviewers, or with the audience for your presentation: Eye contact helps take the fear away from the speaker by getting the audience closer to him. Stress is mainly a result of being with the unknown and uncontrollable.

   Eye contact gives the speaker a picture of the reality that is the audience. It also helps in getting the attention of the audience.

Never Lose Your SWAGGER

3. **Change Your Inner Voice:** Most of us have a critical inner voice that tells us we're stupid, not good enough, that we're too fat, thin, loud, quiet… Being able to change that inner voice is key to feeling self-confident on the inside, which will help you project your confidence to the world. Make your inner voice a supportive friend who knows you fully but also recognizes your talents and gifts, and wants you to make the best of yourself.

   You still want to be able to hear the message, so don't make it so chilled and laid back that you never take any notice of it. You can even choose 2, 3 or as many voices as you want for different occasions. Your voice should always support you, always be helpful, never aggressive and it never puts you down.

4. **Forget Other People's Standards:** Whatever the situation that's causing you a crisis of self-confidence; you can help yourself immeasurably by holding yourself to your own standards alone. Other people have different values from you, and however hard you try, you'll never please everyone all of the time.

   Don't worry that people will think you're too overweight, underweight, too feckless, too boring, too frugal, too frivolous … hold yourself to your standards, not some imagined standards belonging to others. And remember that commonly-held values and standards vary from society to society: you don't have to accept them just because the people around you do.

   People's values define what they want personally, but morals define what the society around those people want for them. Certain behaviors are considered to be desirable by a given society, while others are considered to be undesirable. For the most part, however, morals are not written in stone, or proclaimed by God above, but instead reflect local sensibilities.

   Different societies have different ideas about what is acceptable and not acceptable.

Never Lose Your SWAGGER

5. **Make The Most Of Your Appearance:** Even if you've only got a minute or two, duck into the bathroom to make sure you're looking your best. Brushing your hair, giving your face a good wash, straightening your collar, checking you've not got a bit of parsley stuck between your teeth ... all of these can make the difference between feeling confident in your physical appearance and feeling anxious about an imagined flaw.

   Perfect your physical appearance: There's no denying that one's grooming plays a crucial role in building confidence. Although we know what's on the inside is what truly counts, your physical appearance will be the first to create an impression with the people you meet.

6. **Pray Or Meditate Briefly:** If you believe in a higher power, whether God, or another spiritual force, it can be a real boost to self-confidence to say a silent prayer. (You could also meditate instead of praying.) This helps you to take a step back from your immediate situation, to see the wider picture and to seek help from something or someone greater than yourself.

   This is a Christian prayer, but you could write something similar that fits your own religious beliefs or spiritual tradition.

   Dear God, thank you that you love and accept me as I am ... please help me to do the same ... and help me to grow to become the person you want me to be so that my God-confidence and self-confidence will increase greatly—all for the glory of your name and not mine. Thank you for hearing and answering my prayer. Amen.

7. **Reframe:** If something unexpected happens, it's easy to let it knock your fledgling self-confidence. Perhaps you spill your drink on someone, you arrive late for the big meeting because of traffic problems, or someone who you wanted to speak to gives you a cold brush-off.

   Try to "reframe" the situation; put it in the best possible light: often, events are only negative because of the meaning we attach to them.

8. **Find The Next Step:** Keep your self-confidence up by taking gradual steps forwards, rather than freezing when faced with what seems like a giant leap. If you're not sure what to do, look for one simple step that you can take to make progress.

   That might mean making eye contact at a party, introducing yourself to a stranger, breaking the ice in a meeting, or asking a question of your interviewers that shows your knowledge of their industry and company.

   Start taking action even if you don't have a clear idea of what needs to be done. Start moving towards your goal. Make corrections later.

9. **Speak Slowly:** An easy tip for both seeming and being more self-confidence is to speak slowly. If you gabble, you'll end up feeling worse as you know you're being unclear to your audience or to the person you're in a conversation with.

   Speaking slowly gives you the chance to think about what you're going to say next. If you're giving a talk or presentation, pause at the end of phrases and sentences to help your audience take in what you've said.

   A person in authority, with authority, speaks slowly. It shows confidence. A person who feels that he isn't worth listening to will speak quickly, because he doesn't want to keep others waiting on something not worthy of listening to.

Never Lose Your SWAGGER

10. **<u>Contribute Something:</u>** Have you ever sat through an entire class at college or meeting at work without saying a word? Have you had an evening out where friends chatted happily while you sat and stared silently at your drink?

    Chances are, you weren't feeling very self-confident at the time – and you probably felt even worse afterwards. Whatever the situation you're in, make an effort to contribute. Even if you don't think you have much to say, your thoughts and perspective are valuable to those around you.

    By making an effort to speak up at least once in every group discussion, you'll become a better public speaker, more confident in your own thoughts, and recognized as a leader by your peers. Do you find yourself lacking in self-confidence at times?

    How do you cope with these situations?

Never Lose Your SWAGGER

SWAGGER DISCOVERY

A male is defined as "relating or belonging to the sex that produces sperm to fertilize female eggs".

A man is defined as "an adult male human being".

According to the definition of male provided above, a male's sole purpose in life is to assure the perpetuation of his species.

The male animal also has a strong instinct to hunt and provide. Just take a look at how male animals hunt and bring home food for their brood.

They think nothing of killing and the way that they defend their territory is indeed barbaric.

We see examples of males today. These are guys who think that they need to beat their chest, make women weak, are physically aggressive and discount the opinions of all those who differ from them.

Being a man does not mean eliminating the behaviors that make guys, guys. It just means funneling and tempering the basic instinctual behaviors we are given at birth with other qualities such as rationality and compassion in order to function in today's society.

Never Lose Your SWAGGER

Let us take as an example, the guy who is a player and treats women as sex objects. These are the guys who look at women as conquests or notches on their belt. They are acting in a manner that defines them as a **male** but not as a **human man**. No feeling but an activity that is ruled entirely by testosterone.

Sex is very important to both males and men. The difference is that males do it only to procreate and **men** choose to engage in it with the **woman he loves**.

A man may fantasize about sex but will not act out on those thoughts. A true man will physically engage in sex **only** with a woman he cares about.

Another example is the male who is ready at a moment's notice to answer any real or perceived threat with excessive physical aggression. A mature man will try to appeal to reason first in order to protect the people he cares about and/or himself.

There is not a man on this planet who when he has his back against the wall, will not counter with physical aggression when he thinks there is no other way out.

A male will use it as a primary weapon to get what he wants. A man will have the same goal of protection or the need to protect territory but will use tactics that will not cause mental or physical harm to another human being unless the situation demands otherwise.

There is a misconception today that a guy has to either be the bad boy (male) or has to roll over and act like a wimp. There **is** a middle ground. That middle ground is pairing the higher intelligence that was given to the human male with basic instinct resulting in a man who is a fully functioning "adult human being" rather than as a member of a sex that is only here to produce sperm.

Never Lose Your SWAGGER

GETTING YOUR SWAGGER BACK

W e've all been through it. I'm talking about that rut, funk, spell or period in our lives where we feel like we've lost our swagger.

It is time to take your life BACK!

There are many reasons why this loss in confidence occurs (I'll let you fill in the blanks), but when it happens to you, it sucks. Here are 30 tips to get you out of your rut and help you get your swagger back.

Some say to get a tattoo, go sky diving, shave your head, change your name, throw out all your clothes, move back to your home town, have a one-night-stand and things of that nature, but I want to focus on less extreme measures and more of the simple things you can do.

If you think about it, when an NBA player is in a slump, they're always told to get a few easy layups in or to get to the free throw line to get them going. These types of things should be no different for you.

You don't need to necessarily overhaul everything you do. Sometimes you just have to do the little things that make a big difference to get you going again.

TAKE A GOOD HARD LOOK IN THE MIRROR

1. **Improve Your Diet:** Like the old adage says, "You are, what you eat. "Take out Rockstar, add in water. Take out beef, add in fish or chicken. Take out the M&M's, add in vitamins. Take out McDonald's, add in Subway. You get the point.

2. **Get More Sleep:** Not only will it make you feel more refreshed, but it helps in so many other countless ways. Here's a great article about the importance of sleep.

3. **Get To The Dentist:** Now is not the time to reschedule that appointment. Get your teeth cleaned, crowns fixed, bridges built, and root canals dug. You'll be smiling before you know it.

4. **Get A Haircut:** Okay there's nothing wrong with those Supercuts $14 specials, but it just won't do this time. I'm not saying go to one of those foofy salons where they serve you wine, but just go find a reputable shop and get a nice cut.

5. **Update Your Wardrobe:** I'm definitely not recommending you go splurge on ridiculous items, but sometimes when you look good, you just tend to feel good.

   Treat yourself to a new outfit, but remember to stick to buying pieces that you will always have a need for like a suit for work or wool sweater and leave the trendy new stuff for the fashionistas.

   Here's a book I personally recommend: The Handbook of Style: A Man's Guide to Looking Good

6. **Get A New Pair Of Glasses:** Update your look with a fresh or modern pair of specs. If you're tired of wearing glasses then try contact lenses.

7. **Shine Your Shoes:** Don't use the fake liquid shine stuff. Use real shoe polish, some water and a lot of elbow grease. If you can't see your reflection on the shoe when you're done, then get them shined by a professional.
8. **Buy New Cologne:** The goal here is not to smell like teen spirit. Sample more than a few scents and ask the sales person for their recommendation.

9. **Bring Your Suits To The Tailor:** It might cost you a few bucks, but there is simply no substitute for well-fitting clothes (even better if you can swing a made-to-measure suit).

10. **Wear Your Favorite Underwear:** If you don't have one, get one. If you can't decide between boxers or briefs, go with boxer briefs.

11. **Wash Your Car:** There's something about arriving in style that never seems to get old (even better if you get your car detailed).

12. **Get A New Watch:** It's time to retire that Fossil of a watch and get a true timepiece. Skip the brands that also make clothes and opt for those that only specialize in making watches exclusively.

13. **Stop Comparing Yourself To Others:** This is easy to say and difficult to do, but it is essential in getting your swagger back.

GET YOUR STUFF TOGETHER

14. **Align Your Priorities:** Take a piece of scratch paper out and identify what is important to you in your life right now. Make sure you put yourself as #1.

15. **Set Goals:** You don't have to wait for the new year to set goals.

Never Lose Your SWAGGER

16. **<u>Take Care Of Business At Work</u>**: You spend roughly 60% of your waking life there so make sure you're doing what you need to be successful.

    If you don't like your current job, then quit and find a new one.

17. **<u>Organize Your Finances:</u>** Read "What Every Guy Ought to Know About Proper Money Management." If you need more assistance, make an appointment to meet with a financial adviser.

18. **<u>Drop Bad Habits And Develop Good Ones:</u>** They say it only takes 9 days to form a habit. Do you really need another reason to stop biting your nails already? Start by stopping today.

19. **<u>Cut Dead Weight:</u>** Let go of anything and everything that is weighing you down. This includes extra pounds, negative friends and the subscription to that magazine you never read.

BE MORE ACTIVE

20. **<u>Change Your Latitude:</u>** Take a trip to somewhere you've never been. Traveling often opens up our eyes and changes our perspective (even better if you can afford to go international). There are lots of great deals and it doesn't have to cost too much.

21. **<u>Hit The Gym:</u>** Exercising makes you look and feel better (duh, right?).

22. **<u>Start Running:</u>** Running doesn't require a gym membership and is also one of the best ways to get in shape.

23. **<u>Take Up A New Hobby:</u>** Even if you're already a skilled juggler, you can still always learn a few new tricks.

Never Lose Your SWAGGER

24. **Join A Public Sports League:** They have all sorts of different leagues with sports ranging from kickball to bowling to basketball.

   This is a great way to get in shape and meet new people at the same time.

25. **Learn A New Language:** This is a great way to flex your brain and to challenge yourself. I recommend taking it at a community college or online.

GET INSPIRED

26. **Get Nostalgic:** Get out your old football highlight reel, dust off your trophies, and pull out pictures of your hot ex-girlfriends.

   We're not saying to live in the past, but it's always good to give yourself some credit and remind yourself that you were at one point in time on top of your game.

27. **Listen To Music That Gets You Going:** Check out some of these songs: "The Top 15 Songs to Get You Pumped Up."

28. **Watch Your Favorite Movies Of All Time:** Grab some popcorn and watch that go-to movie that always seems to make you feel alive.

29. **Bring Your Friends And Family Closer:** When your confidence is low, there's nothing like allowing your biggest supporters to give you that much needed pep talk to lift your spirits.

30. **Rekindle Some Of Those Lost Dreams:** It's never too late to go after your dreams. Here are two videos that remind us that anything is possible: "The Inspiration behind Rocky" and "The Best Speech I've Ever Heard Steve Jobs Give."

Never Lose Your SWAGGER

You may find that these won't all work for you, but that's okay. The key ingredient here is to take action and to truly believe in yourself.

SWAGGER

INTELLECTUALISM: THE BRAIN

"Men and women are not prisoners of fate,
but only prisoners of their own minds.

- Franklin D. Roosevelt

I f you are an upwardly mobile individual, you may have wondered from time to time, how does one know that he is educated?

In other words, what are the marks of an educated man? Here are some of the marks that I have observed about truly knowledgeable people or those considered truly educated:

First, they have a healthy and humble respect and reverence for Almighty God. This principle of an educated man is found in the Book of Wisdom, which is the book of Proverbs in the Holy Bible. The verse reads: "The fear of the Lord is the beginning of knowledge."

A person who does not acknowledge and reverence God Almighty is not considered a wise or educated man.

In fact, God considers him a fool.

Never Lose Your SWAGGER

"He is ignorant and knows nothing." No matter how many years of schooling he has behind him, if he does not recognize and respect and fear Almighty God, he is a fool according to the Word of God.

"The fool hath said in his heart, There is no God."

--Psalm 14:1a

There is an old Negro saying that also comes to mind here: **"Education without salvation is damnation."** The other day I saw a very striking sign at a church. It read:

> The dead atheist
>
> The dead agnostic
>
> And the dead saint
>
> All believe God exists now.

A **second** mark of an educated man is that he is humble enough to admit his ignorance.

He realizes that no matter how much he learns, he will never learn or know everything.

Third, a truly educated man continues his education long after his years in high school and college.

He learns until he dies. In the words of Quincy Jones: **"He grows until he goes."**

Another mark of a truly educated man is that he is authentic. He is an original. He is for real. He is himself. He knows he does not have to be like anyone else.

He is therefore original in his thinking, his speaking, and his writing. An educated man is normally very comfortable with himself as well as with others. One commentator uses this phrase:

"He is comfortable in his own skin." I like it.

Another mark of an educated man is that he uses his education and knowledge for wise and good purposes. Of course, he uses it to generate a living for himself and his family. Not only for that but he also uses it to help others who are less fortunate than himself.

Sixth, (to me) one of the greatest marks of an educated man is the ability to express himself clearly through his speech and through his writing.

Then, an educated man is a disciplined man. A disciplined man is willing and able to **"do the worst first".** He is willing and ready to tackle the difficult jobs and tasks even when he does not feel like doing them. Eighth, the educated man exudes an inexplicable quiet confidence about himself.

He is not loud, boisterous or arrogant. But you somehow get the feeling that he knows what he is doing. He normally does not say much, but you somehow sense that if he does say something, it would be important, weighty and worth listening to.

Ninth, the educated man is not a perfect man, but he strives to be a moral man.

He has a strong sense of what is right and wrong. And it is his aim to do the right thing. Because of this, he normally finds favor in the sight of God and man.

Finally, another mark of an educated man is that he understands **etiquette** and **protocol.**

In other words, not only is he smart; he knows how to look smart as well. He knows what to say in different settings. He knows how to act at a backyard barbecue as well as at a stately dinner. He dresses and acts appropriately on any given occasion. I strongly suggest that you strive to be this kind of man.

FOR THE EDUCATED BLACK MAN

"It is part of the function of education to help us escape - not from our own time, for we are bound by that - but from the intellectual and emotional limitations of our own time."

--T. S. Eliot, poet

"Education is an ornament in prosperity and a refuge in adversity."

--Aristotle, philosopher

Never Lose Your SWAGGER

"Nothing is more important than a good education."

--Roy Wilkins

"Without education you are not going anywhere in this world. Education is the passport to our future."

--Selected

"He who opens a school door, closes a prison."

--Victor Hugo

"Human history becomes more and more a race between education and catastrophe."

UNLEASH YOUR BRILLIANCE IN THREE STEPS

1. **Ask A Question:** Grab a fresh sheet of paper or digital document, and write the specific question you're trying to answer at the top. This deliberate start to brainstorming helps focus your mind and lets you begin to get curious about the answer.

   Remember, be specific. For example, instead of "How can I build a better mouse trap?" ask "How can I build a mouse trap that catches twice as many mice, is easier to use, and people will gladly pay twice as much for?"

2. **Brainstorm Ideas:** Now just start writing down possible answers. Brainstorm! Don't censor yourself at all. Write every idea down. You've got to work on impulse and don't allow your inner critic, or rational side, to process the answers.

   At first you'll likely write a lot of obvious answers that also have obvious flaws to them.

   They're probably too risky, too expensive, too slow or flawed in some other way. But as you keep rapidly writing, you'll start putting down zany ideas that are too crazy to work, like finding a magic lantern, or robbing a bank.

   When you keep at it, you'll eventually start getting ideas that seem zany at first, but then reveal themselves to be really clever, unique solutions to that specific problem. You might solve your problem in the first brainstorm, but if not, go on to the next step.

3. **Repeat Daily:** This is where you unleash the power of your subconscious mind. Each day for the next few days, or week or month (whatever it takes), sit down and brainstorm for another 5 minutes. Again, just throw down as many crazy ideas as you can for answering the question you posed at the top of the page.

   Each day you that do this, you'll benefit from the work your subconscious has done on the problem during the previous 24 hours. Even your sleep time is productive for creative problem solving. Very clever recent studies have shown how sleeping on a problem increases leaps of insight.

   Also, each day that you do this, you're encouraging your subconscious to look into the problem further, and you increase the odds that a brilliant flash of insight will hit you sometime when you least expect it.

Never Lose Your SWAGGER

4. **Bonus Strategy:** If you're really having trouble generating fresh ideas, it might be you're just too stuck in repetitive thinking about this topic. One way to break out of your old patterns of thinking and generate new ideas is to take in very random stimulus and try to apply it to the solution.

   You might randomly open a dictionary (or any book), point your finger somewhere on the page and see if you can take that work or phrase and use it in the solution somehow. So what if it's ridiculous! Write it down.

   It's stretching your thinking and helping you transition into that really creative way of thinking. You can also do this by flipping channels, flipping pages of a magazine, finding 'objects' in clouds, or visiting a toy store or museum.

Never Lose Your SWAGGER

THE SWAGGER KISS: BRILLIANCE

E verything we do in life communicates a message to others. An effective interaction tool is to **Keep It Simple and Straightforward**.

This skill makes use of the fact that less is often more, and that good communication should be efficient as well as effective. It doesn't waste time conveying information that isn't prudent (or waste the listener or reader's time).

Too often, people keep talking or writing because they think that by saying more, they'll surely cover all the points. Often however, all they do is confuse the people they're communicating with.

When one is straightforward and honest, situations are met head-on and important issues aren't swept under the rug. There are no elephants in the room!

With a (genuine) straight shooter, "what you see is what you get". They are a frank and honest person and someone who tells it like it is without the sugar coating, but they always come from love.

They sincerely want the best for you, even if they sometimes "seem" brutally honest. If ever you desire or need a straightforward answer, this is the person you need to search out.

Never Lose Your SWAGGER

(Strangely) this interpersonal skill may be one of those things that you'll only really notice when someone doesn't possess it!

Being straightforward in your approach to life is a breath of fresh air for most people. They see you as someone they can trust and they always know where you stand. If you want to be **grow**, **prosper**, and **enjoy life**, **establishing this characteristic is essential**.

When people use direct communication, there is less chance of a misunderstanding, yet there is the possibility for offending or surprising the receiver by the directness/candidness of the disclosure.

So, this characteristic may not please everyone. - PS: this form of direct communication may have little or no effect if the receiver is a person who is very unwilling to listen to you, or anyone else for that matter.

Bill Cosby once shared this bit of wisdom. He said there are many ways to succeed, but **"the key to failure is trying to please everybody."** Realistically, there are some people we just can't please. Or they just don't like you.

Please, don't take it personally, as there are so many reasons involved in why someone likes or dislikes you. However, one does need to be aware of when not to change ones values or beliefs just to please someone else, or perhaps when to move on.

It has been said that friends are the family we choose for ourselves. Each time you use simple and effective communication skills you open yourself to opportunities and future friendships.

By being and surrounding yourself with such dynamic personalities, you're bound to discover and nurture your very best qualities. We all come into this life as diamonds in the rough.

The cut gives a diamond its brightness that seems to come from its very center or heart, and which leads to its brilliance. Now is the time to use our innate abilities and talents and be a diamond cut to maximize our brilliance!

EXTREMELY IMPORTANT DISTINCTIONS BETWEEN INTELLECTUAL POWER AND BRAIN POWER

First of all it is important to understand that the human brain and the mind are not the same things.

Both the mind and mind power are purely a non-physical aspect of you capable only of processing pure consciousness (unseen or spiritual), while the brain is the physical tool that the mind utilizes to process the thoughts derived from consciousness.

This enables the manifestation or the physical appearance of the thing thought of (the ideal) in the physical world.

It has been found that the average person utilizes only 10% or less of their brains capability. What about the other 90%? Would our Creator (Source) have provided us with physical resources and attributes that he/she/it had no intention for us to use?

Is it possible that by becoming consciously aware of the "True Power" of your mind, the fact that human mind power is "Infinite" in nature limited only by a lack of awareness and understanding concerning it's "true" capability that you would become enabled and empowered to begin "consciously" creating desired outcomes in each and every area of your life?

As the spiritual masters, texts and sages have claimed and taught for thousands of years as well as the recent discoveries made through advanced science the answer to that question is... Absolutely!

Once individual human mind power is fully understood and you are made aware of its "infinite" nature, is it possible that the brains ability to expand its function at much greater capacity than most "perceive" to be possible would enable you to dramatically increase outcomes, providing far more "desired" results with far less "physical effort" than what you currently perceive as "logical" or "practical" in the physical world?

Again, as the spiritual masters, texts and sages have claimed and taught for thousands of years as well as the most recent cutting edge discoveries made through advanced science the answer to that question is... Yes!

Never Lose Your SWAGGER

So, how do you begin utilizing this mind power in a way that produces desired results and establish the necessary belief of your ability to do so?

Those are valid and important questions and ones that we will cover here. A willingness to discover the answers to those questions will assist you in developing a heightened awareness concerning how the brain operates.

It will also help you consciously harmonize and utilize your mind power to dramatically increase the brains limitless capabilities.

And you'll get specific steps that you can follow to effectively utilize this increased capability to bring into your life unrealized dreams, desires and circumstances that up until this point, you may have considered to be out of your reach.

By developing an awareness of the functions of the human mind, and establishing a solid belief of your ability to do so, it is possible to consciously and purposefully utilize human mind power to dramatically enhance any area of your life.

That includes financially, in your relationships, physical healing, as well as the capability to develop and dramatically enhance intuitive ability, and a host of other outcomes which fall outside the scope of what is perceived as logical or "possible" based on a strictly and very limited physical perspective.

While many are to some extent, vaguely aware of these capabilities, it seems that few take the initiative to develop the depth of awareness necessary to fully utilize and put their individual mind power to work in their everyday lives, which would enable them to attract and experience what it is that they claim that they have a desire to experience.

The only thing that separates the ultra-successful from the poor is a matter of conscious awareness, choice and/or belief.

The only difference in someone who has psychic ability and one who does not is a lack of awareness of the principles that allow it to develop, as well as a single, or multiple self-limiting beliefs that they can attain such a feat, or the lack of focused and intentional action necessary to make it possible.

The only difference in one's ability to heal the physical body from another's inability is a lack of conscious awareness and belief (faith) in one's ability to do so, or the absence of "focused and intentional action" that would allow it to occur.

From a more physical perspective, the only thing that separates a muscled up body builder from a 90 lb. weakling is the ability to conceive it as an already existing fact in the mind, an enhanced awareness as to how to accomplish it, a belief that he can, and/or the willingness to take the action necessary to achieve it.

The only thing that limits anyone from accomplishing anything that they can conceive in mind is a missing ingredient from the following equation.

AWARENESS + DESIRE + BELIEF + ACTION = UNLIMITED CAPABILITY

Everything that our Creator or Source has provided us with is complicated and limited only by our analytical thought processes and pre-established beliefs that such things must be difficult or in some cases impossible to achieve.

The bottom line is, regardless of what actions you take individually, the process ALWAYS without fail begins at the level of consciousness which is why it is so important for those desiring a greater quality of life to develop and begin to consciously utilize your mind.

Although man has successfully made this extremely simple concept appear to be extremely complex and out of reach of the average person, there are proven and simple means of developing the human mind to consciously and consistently achieve and experience what most would refer to as miracles.

There are very basic Universal principles (Spiritual Laws, Natural Laws, Laws of Nature) as well as scientific studies that support and have proven that the average human does have the ability to consciously create desired outcomes through mind power.

In fact, unbeknownst to many, they already ARE creating each and every event, condition and circumstance that they are currently experiencing in their lives, but due to a lack of deeper understanding or "Awareness" most are doing so "unconsciously."

Becoming Aware of and developing the Understanding of exactly how these basic principles operate, and becoming consciously aware of their unwavering, immutable and predictable nature, combined with establishing the awareness of your ability to harmonize your individual intellectual power with their unfailing nature, are the first steps toward realizing your own true potential and power to become a conscious and purposeful creator of the events, conditions and circumstances which make up your life.

This deeper understanding and awareness will allow you to create for yourself the circumstances that allow you to prosper and experience indescribable fulfillment, (in both the mental and physical realms) and begin to experience and enjoy the kind of life that you were created to live.

You were meant to live a life of joy, fulfillment, inner peace, abundance, and happiness.

SWAGGER CREATIVITY: HERE TO MAKE A DIFFERENCE

C reativity can save the world. Creativity can save your life. Yes it's that powerful. It can make you a millionaire and enchant the lover of your dreams.

It can also take you around the world and fill your days with joy and wonder.

Creativity is one of the most in-demand skills required for the jobs of tomorrow and yet we get almost no creativity training in school.

It's expected that you either have it, or you don't. Read on to find a simple method to begin unleashing your own creative brilliance.

THE INCREDIBLE POWER OF CREATIVITY

First, let's take a moment to look at the value of creativity. I consider creativity one of the biggest keys to living an extraordinary life. Creativity is essentially the ability to think about things in a new way; to take the available resources and find new ways to use them.

It can be used in a variety of artistic ways to create profound new experiences for you and your audience.

It can also be used to solve difficult problems like how to design an amazing new product, how to get out of debt, how to cure malaria or how to arrange the most memorable, romantic date ever.

Whenever you have a goal, creativity can help you figure out how to get from here to there faster, cheaper and easier. If you think about it, there are really very few completely unbreakable laws in the universe.

Strictly speaking there are a handful of things like gravity, the speed of light and so on. With so few real limitations, we really we have enormous freedom to use our skills, time and resources to accomplish amazing things. We just have to figure out how.

And that's where creativity comes in. In fact, I think if someone could figure out exactly the right things to do and say, they could even bring about world peace within 30 days. Think about it…

Everyone has enormous creative potential; they just haven't learned how to unleash it. There is a simple process you can use that overcomes the 3 most common creativity mistakes so you can generate powerful ideas toward whatever goals you're working on.

Let's examine the 3 mistakes:

3 COMMON CREATIVITY MISTAKES

1. **Lack of Focus:** Some people generate lots of great ideas but because they're not directed, they can't be used to accomplish anything meaningful. At other times, people set out to generate ideas without being really clear about what they're trying to achieve. For example, if you sit down to brainstorm "How can I make more money?" then "pan handling" would be a valid solution.

    Much better results would come from a focused question like, "How can I increase my income by 50% within 12 months?"

2. **Lack Of Time:** Like any activity, creativity takes concentrated effort. Thinking takes time. But most people don't sit down and spend the time to actively brainstorm solutions to problems.

   In fact, this is a big difference between experts and amateurs for many different activities.
   The experts often spend more time on projects than amateurs. Don't worry about not having the time to brainstorm. Make time. Brainstorming solutions to life's problems pays for itself by giving you the ability to rapidly solve problems.

3. **Lack of Subconscious Processing:** It's important to recognize that the mind continues to work on problems even when you think you're doing something else. Many famous geniuses have written about this phenomenon and how they used it. It's pretty common for amazing solutions to problems to just pop into someone's mind hours or days later when they're taking a walk, sleeping, showering or doing just about anything.

   But you have to "prime the pump" and give it time to work. Now let's get to the process that allows you to do that.

With an understanding of the three common mistakes responsible for stifling creativity, you can overcome them and become more creative today.

Never Lose Your SWAGGER

AN ALPHA MAN: THE SWAGGER

What does the term alpha male or the alpha man mean to you? What image springs to mind?

Think John Wayne, the epitome of rugged masculinity and an enduring American icon or perhaps other popular iconic figures such as Clint Eastwood, Elvis Presley, Frank Sinatra or Denzel Washington.

Maybe you think of a statesman or world leader like US President Barack Obama or perhaps a legendary sporting hero such as Muhammad Ali or Football (Soccer) coach Jose Mourinho.

Whoever you think of, the alpha male in its simplest form is the most dominant member of group of males to which the others follow. He is a man with power, a natural leader and somebody who projects confidence.

He is positive, articulate and successful, both admired and desired with the ability to effortlessly draw people to him with his charm. He can entertain and inspire all and is the central figure in his interactions with others whatever the environment or social setting.

He doesn't try to be the dominant male, he just is.

Never Lose Your SWAGGER

But power, popularity, happiness, love, success, influence, being desired and admired are all outcomes and the result of actions, personality, passions, skills and experiences.

For some, these outcomes don't happen naturally, easily or at all; instead loneliness, depression, low self-esteem, anger are all too often their unwanted reality.

So what traits manufacture such positive outcomes? Look at the men that you admire the most and you would almost certainly find that they all embody common characteristics that form a blue print for success and happiness that all can follow, learn from and enjoy.

So what are they?

1. **Strength Of Character:** Character distinguishes you from others; it is your attributes, abilities and knowing your own values and morals. Confidence in your character helps you to maintain it and grants you the strength and the ability to resist attacks on it from others enabling you to be unconcerned as to what others think of you.

   It is self-perpetuating and strengthens your inner core. It also helps you to fashion your own identity, builds integrity and has the ability to positively influence others.

2. **Integrity:** Integrity is an adherence to your moral principles. It is honesty and the consistency of your actions, values and methods. This is built from a complete and settled inner sense of yourself and your character. Someone with integrity is able to build trust and respect with others, and build long-term relationships.

   It attracts people of a similar personality and opens the doors of opportunity.

3. **Rational Thinker:** A man who is a rational and a logical thinker is more likely to succeed and make informed choices and decisions than that of someone who reacts with a rash, knee-jerk emotional response to most situations.

Never Lose Your SWAGGER

Emotions are one of our most basic survival mechanisms and help us to identify the threats and opportunities to our emotional well-being.

However, those who are not in control of their emotions are more likely to take unnecessary risks, make bad judgments, alienate or harm others and display negative behaviors such as blame shifting, point scoring (in arguments), intimidation, manipulation, jealousy and aggression.

Someone who is in control of their emotions has the ability to evaluate any given situation taking into account the wider picture from different perspectives. These qualities enable successful and positive decision-making for both short term and long term success.

4. **Self-Aware:** An alpha male knows who he is his values, goals, motivations, passions, strengths and weaknesses and understands how these determine his actions and decisions. This grants him the freedom and opportunity to take control of his own life and not let others, who don't have his best interests at heart, direct his path or well-being.

   Self-awareness breeds confidence, clarity of mind and can relive anxiety and stress.

5. **Charismatic:** Charisma is sexy it builds rapport and relationships. Someone who is charismatic is controlled, self-confident, interesting and an excellent communicator.

   They have the ability to persuade or influence others in a personal and direct manner.

Never Lose Your SWAGGER

Swagger Attracts Opportunities To You

Do you want to find a career that is fulfilling and fully utilizes your talents? Do you want to start that business for which you are passionate?

The key to attracting success is having the confidence to act in a way that is consistent with the authentic person in you. This is your swagger.

Whether you are trying to find what makes you unique or you feel that you have lost touch with the person you truly are over the years, Swagger can help find and integrate the authentic you into your professional life.

THE ART OF GENTLEMANLY ETIQUETTE – PART I

O ne only needs to take a quick glance around to notice that there are very few true gentlemen remaining among us.

In times past, a gentleman was much appreciated and being gentlemanly was a noble thing and characteristics of superior quality. Alas, things have changed in today's society; some for the better and some for the worse. One thing that particularly irks me is the lack of good taste and etiquette most guys are guilty of at the turn of this new millennium. There seems to be a depreciation of gentlemen quality.

I'm not saying that men should act like robots and be slaves to etiquette, but some basic good manners will go a long way in helping you during your ascent to the top of the game.

It is called having social grace and social etiquette.

Never Lose Your SWAGGER

What I've done is compile a quick list of tips that will help turn even the most blundering fool into a proper gentleman. Follow these simple tips and I can assure you that people will perceive you as a man of good breeding and taste, hence a man they wish to associate and conduct business with. Not to mention the fact that the ladies are always quite pleased to meet a real gentleman.

GENERAL ETIQUETTE

- **Always Be Polite:** Even if you don't like someone, there is no need to lower yourself to their level. Be polite and courteous; show that you're the better man.

- **Do Not Curse:** Swearing is a big no-no. It shows that you don't have the vocabulary to express your thoughts appropriately. Furthermore, it is always very crude and impolite to be vulgar.

- **Do Not Speak Loudly:** When you speak loudly, it raises the stress level among company. It always implies that you can't reason with people and rely on "brute force" to get your point across. It also draws negative attention to you.

- **Do Not Lose Your Temper:** When you lose your temper, you are showing everyone that you can't control your emotions. If you can't even control yourself, then how can you possibly control anything else? Keep your cool at all times (it won't be easy but it is worth the effort) and people will take positive note of your levelheadedness.

- **Do Not Stare:** Ogling someone is the equivalent of psychological aggression. You don't want to intimidate people for no good reason.

- **Do Not Interrupt:** Let people finish what they are saying before adding your comments. Interrupting others is a sign of poor etiquette and a lack of social skills. If you want to come across as egotistical, you can do so by constantly interrupting.

Never Lose Your SWAGGER

- **Do Not Spit:** A lot of men do this almost subconsciously. Spitting is very crude and not too pretty to look at. Do not spit in public unless you want to look like you were raised in a sewer.

- **Respect Your Elders:** In fact, you should respect others as you would like them to respect you. I am specifying elders because it seems that today, young men think they know it all. Well, they don't. Just think of yourself five years ago... you're much smarter and experienced today, aren't you? Of course, yet you thought you knew it all five years ago.

- **Do Not Laugh At Others' Mistakes:** This is perhaps one of the cruelest things one can do. When you mess up, the last thing you want is for someone not only to bring it to your attention, but to ridicule you.

- **Remove Your Hat Indoors:** This rule seems to have gone out the window these days. You should remove your headwear upon entering a building. Furthermore, never keep your hat on while at the dinner table. It reflects very poor etiquette.

- **Wait For Seating Before Eating:** When sitting down for a meal, you should wait until all the guests are properly seated and ready to commence the meal before eating. Everyone should start dining at the same time; this is a subtle but very important rule.

THE BASICS OF CHIVALRY

In addition to the aforementioned rules, gentlemen (in training) should follow these additional rules when in the presence of a lady.

Chivalry may be on life support, but it is not dead yet.

- **Always Open Doors:** This is perhaps the most basic rule of male etiquette out there. It is also one of the easiest to follow so you have no reason to forget it. Whether she is about to enter your car, restaurant, club, or anyplace with a door, you should always hold it open for her. If there are many doors, then hold them open one after the other.

- **Put On Her Coat:** Always help a lady put on her coat or over - garment. This is a simple but powerful action.

- **Help With Her Seat:** If an unaccompanied lady is sitting next to you, it is important that you help her be seated by pulling her chair out for her and gently pushing it back into place, with the lady seated of course.

- **Give Up Your Seat:** If a lady arrives at the table and there are no available seats, you should stand up and offer yours to her.

- **Stand At Attention:** Always stand when a lady enters or exits the room. This rule has been somewhat relaxed, so you can stand upon entrance but remain seated upon exit. Nonetheless, if you can do both, you should.

- **Give Her Your Arm:** When escorting a lady (that you know) to and from social events, you should offer her your arm. This is a little more intimate, but serves well when walking on uneven ground; especially if she's wearing high heels.

- **Ask If She Needs Anything:** This is one that most guys already do, but helps complete the gentleman in all of us nevertheless. When at social events, make sure to ask the lady if you can get her something to drink (or eat, depending on the event). Show her that you care about her comfort and needs.

Never Lose Your SWAGGER

Gentlemen, if I may call you that, these are the rules of etiquette you should observe in everyday life. Elevate yourself above the rabble and display the mannerisms of a true gentleman. The world will appreciate such a rarity and your career will most definitely benefit from your good manners and savoir-faire.

THE ART OF GENTLEMANLY ETIQUETTE – PART II

W hat do James Bond and Cary Grant have in common? They represent the quintessential gentleman. It's what makes them so charming and beloved.

They are smooth and suave, and know how to behave in every situation.

What do they have that I don't? you must be asking yourself. Nothing, it's just that they read the book on etiquette.

Although one might think they're a staple of a bygone era, true gentlemen never go out of style.

BASIC GOOD MANNERS

- **Don't Flaunt Your Riches:** Nobody likes a braggart. Keep your assets vague if you have to discuss financial matters. You can wear expensive things without blowing your own trumpet.

- **Never Let Others See You Look At Your Watch:** When you're amid company, ask for the time or look at your watch only if you're ready to leave right that instant. When others notice you glancing at the time, it can be interpreted as boredom. Be inconspicuous.

- **Never Groom Yourself In Public:** This includes picking your nose, chewing your nails and picking your teeth. That should only be done in private. Committing these acts overtly is a colossal mark of a lack of class.

- **Be Punctual:** Perhaps the greatest sign of respect, which is what a gentleman is all about, is being on time. Having people wait for you is the equivalent of telling them that you don't care about them.

- **Shake Hands Firmly:** Your handshake should mirror your personality. You want the other person to think of you as someone resolved, concrete and positive. But it shouldn't be a test of your strength; don't hurt them. Your grip should be the same for women.

- **Apply Constant Verbal Grace:** Use "excuse me" or "I beg your pardon" for all occasions. An extension of politeness, you should always use these expressions, whether it's to get someone to move out of your way, to apologize for your upcoming journey to the men's room, or simply to signal your interlocutors that you're about to start a sentence.

- **Tip Well And Discreetly:** Only tip when it's called for, as opposed to those occasions when it's simply awkward (i.e. hospital nurses or business messenger). When you do tip, don't be cheap. Respect the 15% gratuity for restaurant tabs and nothing less than $10 for a significantly useful maître d'.

- **Project High Moral Values:** Even if you know that deep down you're not, appear as if you were virtuous. A real gentleman always comes out of everything smelling like a rose.

PARTY ETIQUETTE

The following tips apply for those occasions when you are venturing out into social events and get-togethers. God forbid you didn't know how to act like the gentleman you are.

- **Acknowledge Your Acquaintances:** Don't play hide & seek with the people you know, even if you don't feel like talking to them. Bite the bullet, initiate the mandatory greetings, and get it over with.

- **Address New Acquaintances By Their Title And Last Name:** Doctor and military ranks are important to the people who have these titles.

  Mr. and Mrs. should be used for the others (if you're unsure about a woman's marital status, use Ms. when addressing her). Wait until they ask you to use their first name before doing so. There's nothing more irritating than someone who uses your first name two minutes after having met you.

- **Look At Your Speaking Partner:** Your attention should always be focused on the person you are talking with. Always look at them when listening as well as when you are in control of the conversation. Again, it's a question of respect.

- **At Dinner, Address Those On Your Left And Right:** Unless it's a frat house keg fest, don't shout across the table -- concentrate on those closest to you. This will keep the proceedings calm and orderly.

- **Never Remove Coat Or Necktie When In Company:** By keeping your clothes on, you show that you consider the other guests important enough for you to remain fashionably tip-top.

Never Lose Your SWAGGER

- **Only Talk When You've Been Formally Introduced:** Which is why the phrases "Have we met?" or "Have we been introduced?" are so handy. If you feel like speaking to somebody, find a person the two of you have in common and arrange a proper introduction.

- **Let Your Social Superiors Address You First:** Unless you are on intimate terms, always let your social superior address you. This may seem archaic, but think of it in modern terms. You see Bill Gates at the party; do you go talk to him? Not unless you want his bodyguard to intervene. It can be clumsy, so arrange an introduction.

FEELING GALLANT?

You know how to act around the ladies, don't you?

- **Never Smoke In The Presence Of A Lady Unless Invited To:** In this age of political correctness it has almost become a given. While she may not ask you to, make sure you do request her permission.

- **Remove The Cigar From Your Lips If A Lady Passes By:** This one is pure common sense. It's a security measure as well as an indicator of high regard.

- **Always Carry A Woman's Packages:** Let's face it; today's women would probably shoot you a puzzled fleeting look, so at least offer to do so. This lets her know you respect her and are courteous enough to inquire as to her comfort.

Finally, while excessive chivalry is what drove Don Quixote to madness; good manners are never uninvited in this era of fast business and faster relationships. Remember that behaving like a gentleman brings out the lady in every woman.

Never Lose Your SWAGGER

THE ART OF GENTLEMANLY ETIQUETTE – PART III

G ood manners and gentlemanly behavior are to your professional image and social life because your most valuable commodity is yourself.

"People, like diamonds, have a basic market value, but it is only after they have been polished that the world will pay their real value."

- William Thourlby

Here are some additional tips on how to gain a competitive edge by using etiquette to demonstrate that you are a true gentleman.

COURTESY & CONSIDERATION

- **Don't Kiss And Tell:** Discretion, honor and integrity are of paramount importance in developing and maintaining your reputation as a gentleman. Details of your love life should remain private.

  Similarly, if a colleague has too much to drink at a party, be discreet. Never break a confidence and don't participate in unkind gossip.

- **Interrupt Politely:** Etiquette dictates that you should never interrupt, but that's not always practical. Interjecting your comments while someone else is speaking is definitely impolite, unless there is an emergency, or other good and valid reason.

  If you must interrupt or leave a conversational group, be sure to say, "excuse me" or "I beg your pardon." Being polite means treating other people's situations, opinions and feelings with respect.

- **Be Prudently Punctual:** It's important to be respectful of people's time. Arrive on time for meetings, business functions and social events. If a meeting is dragging on later in the day than planned, agent will ask if there are any time conflicts. A true gentleman also recognizes when it's time to leave a party.

SUAVE COMMUNICATION

- **Practice Good Etiquette:** Being courteous and respectful extends to how you handle your oral and written communications. Letters and voicemail messages should show that you are well-mannered and professional. In addition, practice e-mail Netiquette and cell phone etiquette.

- **Be A Gracious Guest:** Thank the host at a social or business function. At a company party, always seek out and thank the most senior management in attendance, plus your own boss and the party organizers.

- **Thank Others:** Send handwritten thank-you notes for any gifts you receive, whether they are from suppliers or clients, or even your great-aunt Martha. Thank your server at lunch, the doorman at your building and your colleague who brings in donuts. Recognizing other people's thoughtfulness demonstrates your good breeding.

- **Don't Be Politically Incorrect:** The difference between a gentleman and a boor is class. Show you have it. Avoid off-color jokes and gossip. A few cheap laughs at someone else's expense will tarnish your image, both socially and professionally.

- **Practice Small Talk:** Whether you're at a wedding reception or business conference, how you make conversation will boost the impression of your refinement. Charming conversationalists mentally rehearse small talk on a variety of topics, avoiding religion, politics and sex.

  A gentleman listens attentively, making eye contact, showing interest and graciously drawing other people into a conversation.

GALLANTRY

- **Carry A Handkerchief:** Plan ahead. Have a clean handkerchief in your pocket, especially when you attend a funeral. It's also a great idea to have a hanky handy for a lady friend to dry raindrops or tears.

- **Share Your Umbrella:** It's very gallant to offer your umbrella to a lady. On a chilly evening or if the air conditioning is high, your wife or date might appreciate the loan of your suit jacket and others will notice your thoughtfulness. However, this gesture may be viewed as patronizing in a business setting, so don't do it for a female colleague unless hypothermia is imminent.

- **Cough Thoughtfully:** If you're overcome by a fit of coughing or sneezing, excuse yourself and leave the meeting or dinner table for a few minutes. Return quietly and apologize again as you take your seat.
- **Pay The Bill Discreetly:** When you invite someone for lunch or dinner, accept the bill discreetly and without fanfare. When you're the guest, you may offer to pay your share or to buy the wine but it is ungentlemanly to argue about who will pay the tab.

CIVILITY & SOCIAL SKILLS

- **Maintain Eye Contact:** At a party, maintain eye contact with whomever you are speaking with. You may be the most well-mannered man, but if someone feels you're scanning the room for someone more important to talk to, your image will be shattered.

- **Make Introductions:** Show your good manners when introducing people by telling them more than each other's names. "Hal, I'd like you to meet Phil Brown, he's a pilot with Delta. Phil, this is Hal Black. He recently returned from the Gulf with the military." Many people have difficulty remembering names, and will appreciate your thoughtful manners if you say "George, you remember Alan, don't you?"

Never Lose Your SWAGGER

- **Engage People:** Be gracious. Make conversation with those on the sidelines, particularly at business functions. Your good breeding and kindness will be remembered. Invite people to become involved, whether it's in a group discussion at a conference, a baseball game at the company picnic or a conga line at a wedding reception.

- **Follow The Host's Lead:** At a business dinner or dinner party, don't sit until your host does, and don't begin eating until they have lifted their fork. Wait to drink your wine until your host proposes a toast or takes a sip. Do not smoke until everyone has finished, and then only smoke if it is clearly permitted and once you have asked permission of your tablemates.

TABLE MANNERS

- **Never Speak With Food In Your Mouth:** No one wants to see what you're chewing or listen to you talk with a mouthful of food. If you're asked something and your mouth is full, signal your apologies and, if your dining partners are refined, they will patiently wait until you're able to reply.

  Unless there's a valid reason to wolf down your food and bolt from the table, eat slowly and converse with your tablemates.

- **Don't Reach Across Someone:** When dining with others, don't reach over; politely ask someone to pass the bread. When they do, take the tray or basket and offer the passer a piece of bread before taking one. If the bread is in front of you, pass it to the person beside you and, if they are knowledgeable about good etiquette, they will offer it to you before taking their own.

Never Lose Your SWAGGER

- **Put Down Your Knife:** Unless you're expecting an attack from a pack of marauding wild animals, put down your knife after cutting your food and before eating it. It demonstrates good table manners, slows down the process of eating and allows you more time to showcase your talents as a scintillating conversationalist.

WOMEN & CHIVALRY

- **Open The Door:** In a business context, opening the door for women can be a contentious issue, so don't make it too obvious. If there are men and women in the group, hold the door for everyone. In a social context, a gentleman will always hold the door for a lady.

  In addition, go around to open the car door and wait there until she is seated.

- **Retrieve Dropped Items:** When someone drops something, pick it up and hand it back, whether it's a glove, a file folder or a twenty-dollar bill. Make sure you bend at the knees, not from the waist.

- **Walk Beside A Lady On The Stairs:** Never walk behind a woman on the stairway, especially if she's wearing a miniskirt. Walk beside her or slightly ahead of her on the stairs. When exiting a subway station in a crush of people, a gentleman will avert his eyes from the thighs ahead of him.

  The same principle applies if you are walking on the streets; don't follow any woman you don't know too closely.

- **Walk On The Outside Of A Sidewalk:** This allows your lady to be farther from the traffic. This way, if someone is going to be splashed, it will be you, not her. I know, I know... but that's the price to pay if you want to be a gentleman.

UNCOMMON COURTESY

As author John Bridges says, being a gentleman requires "a little logic, a bit of forethought and a great deal of consideration for others."

Incorporate these tips, and the ones in Part I and Part II, into your daily routine. Think of it as a personal marketing program to showcase your finest features.

Polish your professional and social image, and become recognized and remembered for being a chivalrous, gallant and refined gentleman.

DON'T SETTLE FOR MEDIOCRITY

Recently, I saw some statistics which indicated that about 80 percent of people are living a life of mediocrity.

This means that four out of every five people we encounter are not living up to their true potential.

Og Mandino in his best-selling book, The Greatest Secret in the World, says that "The greatest secret in the world is that you only have to be a small measurable amount better than mediocrity... and you've got it made." Does this mean that most people produce mediocre work, so if we operate at a level just above mediocre we are more likely to attain success?

If that is the case, how do we define mediocrity? Freedictionary.com defines mediocrity as, "ordinariness as a consequence of being average and not outstanding."

Are you living a life of mediocrity?

No one ever says that when I grow up I want to be mediocre, so how did we veer so far off our intended path?

Why do we settle for ordinariness, for mediocrity? Is it because of laziness, low self-esteem, repeated failures, disappointments, feelings of unworthiness and un-deservedness, or because it is comfortable?

I have no answers, but it is something for us to think about and then take action to reduce the statistics.

In The Greatest Salesman in the World, Mandino shares many ideas. Below are five of these ideas worth thinking about because they will direct us on the path to become extraordinary:

1. Master the art of living not for you alone, but for others.

2. No other trade or profession has more opportunity for one to rise from poverty to great wealth than that of a salesman. Anyone could sell all goods if he/she learned and applied the principles and laws of selling.

3. Wealth should never be your goal in life. True wealth is of the heart, not of the purse. Do not aspire for wealth, and labor not only to be rich. Strive instead for happiness, to be loved and to love, and most important, to acquire peace of mind and serenity.

4. Until the fig tree is ripe it cannot be called a fig and until you have been exposed to knowledge and experience you cannot be called a salesman [expert].

5. Never feel shame for trying and failing, for he who has never failed has never tried. Failure will never undertake you if your determination to succeed is strong enough.

Professionals can easily become overwhelmed or even distracted by all the great information that is out there about how to be the best you. But the problem is that the information is "out there" and they do not know what to do with it. They have no idea what the next step should be to apply the information to improve their condition in life.

Keeping Mandino's five ideas in minds, why not take incremental steps to become remarkable? Answer the following questions:

1. What is your mission in life?

2. In the next three years, where would you like to be in your personal and professional life? Frame your responses in the form of goals.

Never Lose Your SWAGGER

3. Are you committed to achieving those goals? Why? Why not?

4. In the past, what has prevented you from achieving your personal and professional goals?

5. Develop strategies in advance to overcome those obstacles.

6. Think about your professional goals, what gaps exist between where you are now, to where you would like to be in the next three years?

7. What actions do you have to take to fill those gaps? Please describe in detail and list your actions in order of priority.

8. What knowledge do you have to acquire to fill those gaps? Please describe in detail.

9. Who are the experts that you can learn from? Secure the books they have written, listen to the interviews and presentation they have given.

10. Start building your body of knowledge based on your mission in life

Take incremental steps to realize your mission in life, and perform an action which takes you closer to your goal each day. You do not have to conform and be like the 80 percent of people who are mediocre. Instead, be the purple cow, the mythical beast that is remarkable.

Never settle for a life of mediocrity.

CHARACTER AND INTEGRITY

To thine own self be true, and it must follow, as the night the day, thou canst not then be false to any man.

--- *(William Shakespeare, 1564-1616).*

It's been said that character is defined by what you do when you think no one is watching.

What an illuminating concept that is.

Most of us have a public face and a private face. There are parts of ourselves we don't want the world to see. Typically, we tend to hide the aspects that would not be viewed favorably by society. Greed, lust, jealousy, pettiness, fears and so on.

We also tend to hide our weaknesses. No one needs to know that we can wolf down a gallon of ice cream in an hour, do they? ;-)

I think most people are "good" at their core; decent, loving, compassionate and kind. However, even those we perceive to be good people are capable of unspeakable acts.

How many times have you heard a convicted murderers' family member or friend say, "I just can't believe he would be capable of something like that. It's so unlike him." The killer projected one identity to the world, while secretly he was someone else entirely.

Okay, most of us are not murderers. Yet, even those of us who would be considered "good people" often think nothing of stealing, cheating on our spouses, or worse. What does that say about our character? Is it wrong only if we get caught?

How many times have you done something that you probably wouldn't have done if others had been there to see it? Would you feel embarrassed if these things were brought to public awareness?

Did you act on your impulses only because you felt sure no one would ever find out?

I've been thinking a lot about the concept of "sin" lately. What is sin exactly? In the Christian religion, sin refers to that which displeases (or dishonors) God. The Ten Commandments warn us against adultery, theft, murder and more. Supposedly if you follow that list, you will remain in God's good graces.

In some earth religions, there is only one commandment: Harm None; which basically covers all angles in two words.

Do nothing that would cause harm to yourself or another. That seems simple enough to follow yet, in both of these examples there are gray areas, aren't there?

Never Lose Your SWAGGER

Sometimes it's hard to tell what's right or wrong. If we find money on the street and pick it up, is that stealing? Does it make a difference if it was $5.00 or $500.00? If we lie to protect someone's feelings, is that wrong?

If we take some paper clips home from the office, is that stealing? Does it "harm" the company, really? If we flirt with someone other than our spouse, or fantasize about them, is that cheating? Or is cheating only the physical act of sexual intercourse?

In situations like these, how do we know the right course of action? How do we balance integrity with our impulses and desires? I think it can help to examine your motives and the possible consequences. What is your intent in this situation?

What do you hope to gain from it? Could your actions harm another, or yourself? If your actions became public knowledge, would you be okay with that?

Maybe some of you are rolling your eyes at me right now, thinking, and "What's the big deal? So what if I take a few things from work, or cheat on my wife? What they don't know won't hurt them." That may be true, but doesn't it hurt you in the long run? Don't those actions detract from the kind of person you are? Don't they dim your inner light?

If it's true that we are all connected, then isn't it also true that harming another means harming ourselves? By disrespecting others, we disrespect ourselves and God.

Personally, I don't believe that God is angry and judgmental, sitting up in the clouds waiting to cast us into the pits of Hell for our transgressions. I do believe there will be a final "review" of our lives, and we will have to answer for the things we've done. But I think we will be our own judges. In the deepest part of ourselves, we know right from wrong.

We're not perfect, and no one is expecting us to be. We all make mistakes and do things we are later ashamed of. We are human, after all. But there is a big difference between making a mistake, and purposely doing something we know is wrong.

Never Lose Your SWAGGER

We may try to fool ourselves at times and justify our actions. Maybe your husband doesn't pay attention to you, so you try to convince yourself that it's okay to have an affair with a man who does. Or your employer gives you a crappy raise, so you decide to make up for it in other ways, like stealing supplies or fudging your time sheet.

They asked for it, right? You certainly have the right to do these things, and probably no one will stop you. Our greatest gift in life is Free Will. Unfortunately, it is also often our greatest curse. There are always consequences to our actions, whether they come now or later.

In the end, it's all a matter of personal accountability. Do we want to be a person of character, or not? It doesn't matter if we get caught or not. What matters is that we are defined by our actions. If I take something that doesn't belong to me, I am a thief. If I cheat on my spouse, I am an adulteress. If I don't want to get caught, I probably shouldn't do these things in the first place. The truth has a way of making itself known.

I can remember as a young man when I lived my life in such a manner that was reckless and wild. It was a time of recklessness and without doubt.

Whether it was wrong or right, pass or fail, up or down, I would at least start and finish. When we are young we make mistakes, then we learn from them, at least the leaders do. Some think that failure is a bad thing, but I truly believe you grow from mistakes, if, you can realize to do that no more.

There are so many gifts inside of us that many of us will never know simply because we are afraid to fail when we are chasing a dream. Fear is a common emotion that hinders our path to our unique creativity, and if allowed, it will steal our dreams. I say allowed only because it's the truth.

I believe when we make our minds up, to not let fear into our mind, we will overcome and that is where victory starts.

Never Lose Your SWAGGER

Look at all the stories out there that started out complete failures, but because of a determination to succeed, and a never give up attitude, ended up becoming someone's story of a dream come true. How many times must one fail? This can only be answered by the desire within to succeed, and the confidence in knowing you are doing the right thing.

Never Lose Your SWAGGER

SEXUALLY APPEALING: SWAGGER SEXY 101

We are more than our sexual appetites; we are a contrast of many features: it is these very same features that make us so sexy.

What makes a man appealing? Is it his dashing good looks? Is it his rock-hard pecks and abs of steel?

Or is it his smile and his personality? In a society where everyone seems aesthetically astute, it's difficult to validate this question for sure.

Sexiness is a very subjective matter and is very relative at that. It holds inconsonant views from each individual just as everyone squabbles over tastes in clothes and food. Hence, a universal answer to this blown-up question is an illusion.

Nonetheless, having met men from all walks of life with radical tastes and personalities, I think I can provide authentic down-to-earth revelations regarding this subject.

So what makes a man sexy?

1. **Masculinity:** There is more to a man than his firm butt and washboard abs. True, what a woman first notices is his anatomical assets but what lingers in her mind is not all that. It's his inherent masculinity. It's in the way he languidly struts across the room with a show of adequacy and grace and the way he flashes the glint in his eyes that ultimately creates the spark. It's also in the manner that he moves and talks that keeps women's eyes riveted at him. Being masculine does not merely suggest flaunting a large build or a protective quality but having this natural instinctive masculine self to trigger women's instinctive feelings of attraction.

2. **Smile:** A natural sweet smile is one of the greatest attractions of a man. It exudes an aura of congeniality and establishes charisma presence. It also breaks a woman's resistance and communicates hidden messages without any verbal language. This is why a man who is generous with his smile is guaranteed to maintain a women-magnet profile!

3. **Eye Contact:** A man who knows how to have eye contact is a man who knows how to communicate. Women just like men are absolute attention seekers. They want men to listen and to take heed of the things they say. Thereupon, they demand affirmation. Eye contact is a way of ratifying. It makes a woman feel sufficiently attended to and cared for. Eye contact makes women feel so extremely special that they tend to sometimes melt right on the spot.

4. **Confidence:** Confidence makes a man. There's just something about the appeal of wealth and power that women can't resist. Antithetical to how most people view it, giving off that commanding vibe isn't always dependent on one's bank account.

   Men can actually take on that aura of authority just by moving through life with an air of self-assurance and a boost of self-esteem.

Never Lose Your SWAGGER

5. **Aromatic Sense:** If a man is a making of a heartthrob onscreen and is a hunk on a ramp but stinks, he definitely goes down the cutthroat world. No woman likes a man who smells a bit too ripe like he just spent 24 hours locked in the bathroom. If a man looks good and smells even better, women are bound to swarm around him.

6. **Sense Of Style:** Some men just don't seem the type to go with the fashion trend. But it does not mean that they are passé. Some just have their own personal preferences and resist the lure of punked-up garments. Actually, it's not the clothes that make a man sexy. It's how he carries his apparel with confidence and ease that does. Clothes don't entice women, it's the man that makes those clothes look good in him that wiles them.

7. **Communication Skills:** Intellect is a factor in today's attraction equation. We are in such a competitive world that anyone without it is immediately slighted. But intellect without communication skills is not an attractive product. Conversational skills are necessary for any man to be a winner.

   He must know when and how to start up a conversation and carry it on 'til it tapers off. He should not patronize women and is not so full of himself. It is believed that if a man is able to stimulate a woman's brain in a conversation, it is likely that he can stimulate her in general.

8. **Sensitivity:** Sensitivity is sexy but too much sensitivity is femininity. So where do we draw the line? When we talk about sensitivity on the right scale, it means having a sense of empathy, confidentiality and trust rolled into one. When a woman confides something, a man's initial reaction is to help her find a solution or fix it himself.

   This is not sensitivity. When a woman expresses her feelings, she just needs an ear to absorb the steam out of her being. A sexy man sees this through and gets women every time.

Never Lose Your SWAGGER

9. **Sense Of Humor:** Laughter releases chemicals that create a sense of well-being, which is a wonderful turn-on. A man equipped with a good sense of humor automatically wins his points on the sexy scale with women. With the mighty use of his expression and wits combined, he becomes an addiction that women just can't get enough of. Women think that if he can evoke them with laughter in public, chances are he can also make them giggle in bed, which is more desirable than it sounds. Women want a man that makes them feel at ease in public and in private.

10. **Oddity:** Extrinsic and intrinsic personal abilities and traits that are considered unique and superior by a woman's biology and also by the society to which she identifies with are, to varying extents, very charming to the female species. If a man has the gift of music or have potential fancy footwork or simply has art at his fingertips, he can charm his way anywhere.

    A mysterious facade that keeps her intrigued and guessing is also deemed bewitching. But a man's resistance to a woman's seduction is considered the prime. Its effects are naturally ingrained into the "sex" part of a woman's brain that it drives her motors purring all the time.

What makes a man sexy is but everything about him and even more. Whether it is on the surface or skin deep, it's just a matter of projection. Every man is sexy in their own ways. They just have to feel that in themselves so the seething sexiness comes out of them naturally.

BRINGING SEXY BACK

In 2006 Justin Timberlake declared that he was bringing "Sexy Back." Prince promptly replied that sexy never left. I'm inclined to side with Prince (though I still love the Justin Timberlake track). So what is sexy?

How do we define sexiness? Is there a difference between the two? And how do they differ from sex appeal? Let's consult the Merriam-Webster dictionary for distinctions:

Sexy: 1 - sexually suggestive or stimulating; erotic. Sexiness is defined as: sexually suggestive or stimulating; erotic...ok...let's define sex appeal: 1 - personal appeal or physical attractiveness especially for members of the opposite sex.

Most women know that men are visual creatures and have sex on the brain. By the way, contrary to popular belief, we don't really think about sex every 7 seconds as Alfred Kinsey once reported. A recently conducted survey found that 54 percent of men think about sex several times a day, according to the National Academy of Scientists.

These stats are interesting, but not important because all men need to know is this: women don't think about - or want - sex as much we do. What would be interesting to note (and what I'd pay money to find out) is how often do women think about their own sex appeal?

Probably just as much if not more than men think about sex.

While men want sex (in general), women want to know that they are sexually appealing (in particular) to the man of their choice. While single, their sexiness gives them an advantage in attracting men in the singles marketplace over their competition.

The sexiest girl in the club is often the one who gets the most attention, but her true sex appeal is not readily known.

More primitive men think of a woman's sex appeal in terms of who they'd most like to have sex with. That form of sex appeal lacks distinction and discrimination.

It's also biological. Men are not hormonally wired for monogamy. Our lecherous ways in fact serve a biological function in the procreation process. Selection conflicts with that process. Our criteria are mind-numbingly simple.

Contrary to what men think, women (even those who are promiscuous) are selective (at least more selective than men).

The cost of having sex and the potential results thereof are much greater for women.

Never Lose Your SWAGGER

Richard F. Taflinger had this to say on the subject in his popular article The Biological Basis of Sex Appeal:

In most species, females bear the brunt of the cost of sex in both time and energy. Among mammals, she must not only produce the young, she must rear them to the point of self-sufficiency.

Thus, unlike the male, she doesn't have the choice of promiscuity, of creating as many offspring as possible as quickly as possible; she cannot abandon offspring as soon as they are born, or her genes die with the infant (Daly 1983).

All this means she must be highly selective in her choice of mates if she wishes to produce the highest quality offspring in her reproductive lifetime. If she selects just any male that comes along, she could waste all the time and energy that pregnancy and rearing require on a possibly weak or nonviable offspring.

Her criteria thus are aimed at getting the best possible male. What is important is the quality of genes he brings and the help, if any, she will have while carrying, bearing and rearing her young.

Her criteria, therefore, are more complex than the male's. Not only must he be physically acceptable, but should satisfy other factors that may contribute to her and her offspring's welfare.

These can include leadership, status within a group, and fighting skill. The sex act, and his participation, being so brief, doesn't have to be of any great interest to her.

He need merely be able to achieve orgasm.

Sex appeal plays a major role in the context of a relationship. The "personal" aspect of sex appeal is a dual process: **1)** relating to one's self in a personal way that speaks to your belief in your physical attractiveness which makes you feel more desirable **2)** relating to one's lover in a way that makes him feel physically attractive.

Two people who feel inner attractiveness and find each other to be highly desirable are very sexy.

Before any of that happens, a huge hurdle must be overcome. A hurdle that often proves to be insurmountable for many women, but is absolutely necessary in achieving true sex appeal: comfort with one's body (including self-diagnosed imperfections) and a healthy attitude about one's sexuality, and sex in general. It's truly a rarity. It's also truly sexy.

Ask any man you know who has experienced this type of sex appeal and they will probably describe it one word: irresistible.

It's also elusive. There are many women who are sexy, but many lack sex appeal.

Tight pants, form-fitting dresses, high skirts, abundance of cleavage, it's all... titillating but it's no indicator of sex appeal; it's merely an attempt at being sexy with the use of skimpy clothing.

At the end of the day (especially at night) evolved men know that women who have sex appeal don't need the help of sexy clothes to showcase it. Their sex appeal comes through - clothed or not. Their sexiness lies within the tangible comfort levels within themselves, and the organic sex appeal which resides there.

That type of sexiness never leaves...or has to be brought back.

WHAT IS HEALTHY SEXUALITY?

- Healthy sexuality involves recognizing that we are all sexual beings, and celebrating the ways that our sexuality benefits us physically, emotionally, and spiritually.

- Healthy sexuality is positive and enriches our lives. Healthy sexuality allows us to enjoy and control our sexual and reproductive behavior without guilt, fear or shame.

- Sexual expression is a form of communication through which we give and receive pleasure and emotion. It has a wide range of possibilities - from sharing fun activities, feelings and thoughts, warm touch or hugs, to physical intimacy. It is expressed both individually and in relationships throughout life.

Never Lose Your SWAGGER

The Healthy Sex "CERTS" Model

Wendy Maltz developed the CERTS model for healthy sex; this model requires that the following conditions be met for a person to enjoy healthy & satisfying sex: Consent, Equality, Respect, Trust, and Safety.

- **CONSENT** means you can freely and comfortably choose whether or not to engage in sexual activity. You are able to stop the activity at any time during the sexual contact. It also means that you respect when someone else does not want to engage in a particular activity, for any reason.

- **EQUALITY** means your sense of personal power is on an equal level with your partner. Neither of you dominates the other.

- **RESPECT** means you have positive regard for yourself and for your partner. You feel respected by your partner and you respect them.

- **TRUST** means you trust your partner on both a physical and emotional level. You have mutual acceptance of vulnerability and an ability to respond to it with sensitivity.

- **SAFETY** means you feel secure and safe within the sexual setting. You are comfortable with and assertive about where, when and how the sexual activity takes place. You feel safe from the possibility of harm, such as unwanted pregnancy, sexually transmitted infection, and physical injury.

It takes spending time together and engaging in lots of honest, open communication to make sure that the CERTS conditions are operating in your relationship. That's why it is helpful to allow all aspects of a relationship to grow and develop at a consistent pace with physical intimacy.

Never Lose Your SWAGGER

Meeting the **CERTS** conditions does not ensure that you'll have amazing sex, but it can help you feel more secure in your relationship and increase your level of self-esteem.

PRACTICE GOOD COMMUNICATION

- Good communication is crucial to healthy sex. You can greatly increase feelings of mutual respect, emotional closeness, and sexual pleasure when you and your partner know how to communicate well with each other. Knowing how to talk openly and comfortably can help you solve sexual problems that come up from time to time in the normal course of an on-going intimate relationship.

- Be patient with yourself and your partner as you work to develop new communication skills. It takes time and a lot of practice to open up emotionally and discuss personal topics in safe and sensitive ways.

STRENGTHEN TRUST

- Trust is an important quality in healthy sex. It helps us feel emotionally safe and secure about choosing to remain in an intimate relationship with our partner. Without trust, we're likely to feel increased amounts of anxiety, fear, disappointment and betrayal.

- Trust grows when both people in the relationship act responsibly and follow-through with commitments. While no one can guarantee that any relationship will last and remain satisfying for both people, you can strengthen mutual trust by having clear understandings about what you expect from each other in the relationship.

Never Lose Your SWAGGER

- Spend time with your partner discussing what you need and expect in the relationship for you to feel emotionally safe. Based on your discussion, create a list of understandings you will both agree to honor. You may want to formalize your list into an actual "contract" you will follow.

HEALTHY SEX COMPARISON CHART

Learning how to distinguish healthy sex from other forms of sex can empower you to bring healthy sex more into your own life. The chart below outlines how healthy sexuality differs from abusive and addictive sex.

Healthy Sex	Unhealthy Sex
Sex is controllable energy	Sex is uncontrollable energy
Sex is a choice	Sex is an obligation
Sex is a natural drive	Sex is addictive
Sex is nurturing, healing	Sex is hurtful
Sex is an expression of love	Sex is a condition of love or devoid of love
Sex is sharing with someone	Sex is "doing to" someone
Sex requires communication	Sex is void of communication
Sex is private	Sex is secretive
Sex is respectful	Sex is exploitative
Sex is honest	Sex is deceitful
Sex is mutual	Sex benefits one person
Sex is intimate	Sex is emotionally distant
Sex is responsible	Sex is irresponsible
Sex is safe	Sex is unsafe

Never Lose Your SWAGGER

Sex has boundaries	Sex has no limits
Sex is empowering	Sex is power over someone
Sex enhances who you really are	Sex requires a double life
Sex reflects your values	Sex compromises your values
Sex enhances self esteem	Sex feels shameful

HUMAN SEXUALITY AND HUMAN RELATIONSHIPS

We are born with a mind that is what it is due to an evolution spanning over billions of years. Reproduction existed before the evolution of sexes. Organisms reproduced through binary and multiple fission (Division).

Evolution of sexes was the result of desire of getting pleasure, joy and happiness out of this ongoing process. What else would result in the evolution of two different sexes as opposed to everyone being same and the survival of species is being successfully achieved by division of organism after reaching a certain stage of development.

This pretty much guaranteed the perpetuity of life if not more, then at least at the same level as the sexual reproduction. Think about it! Even from religious point of view, was it impossible for God to have us reproduce without sex?

Obviously not.

So the creation of sexes was not merely for reproduction, because it could have been achieved without sex and lots and lots of primitive organism still do it asexually just by dividing themselves. So, why did sexes evolved or God created sexes? Apparently the purpose was beyond procreation. Obviously the reason was to add some fun in procreation and perpetuity; to reward ourselves or His creatures for a heavy and difficult responsibility of procreation and raising the newborns and kids.

Another question that arises at this point is why there is so much attraction between opposite or even same sexes, depending on one's preference, not just in human beings but in all bi-sexual animals and may be even in bi-sexual plants.

Some would say for the sake of procreation!

True but how many of us are actually thinking about procreation when attracted by another human being? May be sometimes... some of us. But most of the time we just want to have intimacy and/or sex.

Also, why there is so much fun, joy and pleasure in sex? Again some would say for the sake of procreation. True. But why in most cases this pleasure becomes the sole cause of sex or the sole achievement from sex as opposed to procreation?

Beside, why did even our minds grow so much desire for sex? Why do we even have special centers in our brain that cause desire for sex, sexual attraction and immense pleasure during sex, that becomes the root cause of repeating that experience again and again?

Our sexual behavior is not just effected by evolution and brain, it is also very much shaped by the way we grow up; social, cultural and religious values; incidents and accidents in life etc. etc.

From time when it was OK to have sex with 'anyone', to 'not with family members', to 'not with first relatives'; strictly 'within the bond of marriage', to ' within committed relationships', to 'anyone you like and have consent from'.

We may also have reservations about how often we should have or allow someone to have it from us; some particularly women consider it their right to limit his access regarding how often he can access and how long and how much he can have; they may also consider too much sex as degrading and disgusting for a woman and may think that limited access will keep him interested; this was probably more true in past but now-a-days.

It just frustrates him and since now that more women are accessible to him, he just goes on to 'cheat' or leave her for a 'better, more easily accessible and available option: What is right sex and what is wrong sex; for some anal sex may be a sin and oral sex dirty: How to proceed during sex; some want to do it and get over with it as soon as possible, while others want to take it easy and like to do some romance and foreplay before actually having sex; sex at different ages and stages of life; sex as a lover, spouse, parent etc. etc.:

Childhood circumstances like abuse, incest, early experiences also affect the behavior and approach towards sex and partners. These factors are well known to cause behavioral problems like exaggerated cautions, irrational limits, phobias, paranoia, weird beliefs and myriad of others.

Other factors that affect sex are psychological and physical factors like stress, mood, tiredness, level of excitement, attraction and likeliness towards partner to name a few.

A large number of couples report a sudden change in sexual behavior and lack of interest, particularly in women after becoming a parent. This is, as usual, the result of so many different factors like beliefs, tiredness, stress, divergence of attention and goals of relationship.

Some people, especially women truly believe that mothers are not supposed to have sex or at least they consider it 'disgusting'. Some of them may be too tired and/or stressed by new baby. In other cases the focus of attention is changed from partner to baby and they cannot share this attention with partner anymore. For others, having a baby is the only or most important goal of relationship, particularly for woman.

In this case, she does not have any interest in sex anymore.

Diseases like depression, cardio-vascular problems, erectile dysfunction and painful intercourse may also be causing problems.

Sex is known to cause happiness, satisfaction, pride, lust for life, lowers the blood pressure, reduces risk of cardio-vascular incidents and accidents, and increases life expectancy.

Never Lose Your SWAGGER

Lack of sex or not enough sex is known to cause frustration, depression, shame, suicidal ideation, increased blood pressure, increased risk of cardio-vascular incidents and accidents, and reduces the life-expectancy.

If you and/or your partner/spouse or both of you are experiencing sex related issues then first and foremost important thing is to find out the cause, because remedy depends on cause.

For physical causes like erectile dysfunction, infections and inflammatory disorders, trauma, etc. see your physician ASAP.

For psychiatric problems like depression, phobias, anxiety, panic and bi-polar issues see a Psychiatrist as soon as possible.

You may also realistically find out how much two of you like each other anymore and how much you want to live with each other. Sometimes it may be only religious, cultural, moral, social and/or economic and financial factors keeping you together. You may have to think, discuss and mutually consider, is it really worth to live together and how much? If there is lack of interest, can it be revived and how?

Remembering and recalling the past works sometime. Like how did you meet? How much you liked and loved each other? What did you like about each other? How you have been there for each other under all circumstances. Remembering, talking about and watching the pictures and videos of main events of your life like, your love before marriage, engagement, marriage, honeymoon, birth of a child, etc.

You can also talk about and find out where the flame is still burning? What do you still like about each other? What about him/her still turns you on? What are the reasons you should stay together or the reasons that are keeping you together? Regardless of all the factors, how much this relationship still means to you?

You don't have to focus on positives only. You should also take this as an opportunity to fix the problems. You can talk about or find out about what is turning you/ and/or your partner/ spouse off? What is causing the lake or absence of interest? What you and/or the partner/spouse does not like about his/her spouse/partner? What needs to be changed? What can be and/or should be fixed?

Never Lose Your SWAGGER

Dissatisfaction and/or disappointment may be the cause of problem. What he and/or she expected of this relationship? Was or were those expectations realistic? How many and how much of those were fulfilled?

Are those controllable circumstances? Can that be or needed to be changed or reversed? Are those forgivable or need to be forgiven? Are any of you/Both of you exaggerating and/or misunderstanding, exaggerated and/or misunderstood/ exaggerated something/certain things?

Lack of interest, focus and/or attention is very common cause. Practically speaking this is not spending enough time together. Many factors like work, particularly for men; family and kids, especially for women; in metro areas, long commutes; Too much focus on out of home social life like extended family, friends, sports, clubs, fitness; too much TV, Internet, video games, etc., may cause this problem.

Solution may be seemingly simple and minor but sometimes difficult to practice because of too much occupation of one or both partners with one or more of the above mentioned problems. Solutions may be as simple as just talking every day, watching TV **together**, eating together, Going out together as much as possible, a little vacation time, etc.

Spicing it up a little bit also works, especially for men. A new hairstyle; sexy clothes, lingerie and shoes; his favorite dish; talking on topics of mutual interest, going to bed at same time are known tricks.

Never Lose Your SWAGGER

POSITIVE MENTALITY PRODUCES A POSITIVE FUTURE

Not intended as an exhaustive treatise, but to motivate the reader to believe that, "They themselves are makers of themselves." by the thoughts they encourage.

A person's thoughts form an inner garment of character and an outer garment of circumstance.

THOUGHT & CHARACTER

"As a man thinketh in his heart, so is he". The sum of a man's thoughts is his character. His character influences the conditions and circumstances of his life. Every action springs forth first from thought – even actions considered to be spontaneous and unpremeditated.

Act is the blossom of thought, and joy and suffering are its fruit. The law of **cause** and **effect** exists in the world of thought, not just the natural world. A God-like character is the result of God-like thoughts. A bestial character is the result of groveling thoughts.

Man is made or unmade by his own thoughts, which can destroy him or build him up.

Man becomes master of his "household" of thoughts, by application, self-analysis and experience.

Gold and diamonds are found only by much searching and mining. Similarly, a man must dig deep in the mine of his soul to find every truth connected with his being.

A man must watch, control and alter his thoughts – tracing their effect on himself, others, and his life and circumstances. In doing so he will prove to himself that he is maker of his own character, life and destiny.

EFFECT OF THOUGHT ON CIRCUMSTANCES

A man's mind may be likened to a garden; cultivated or uncultivated. The cultivated garden produces flowers & fruit, while the uncultivated garden produces weeds. A man must continually weed-out all wrong, useless, and impure thoughts and deliberately cultivate right, useful, and pure thoughts.

Thought and character are one, and character has a profound influence on the circumstances of one's life. If a man learns the spiritual lesson of his current circumstances they will give way to other circumstances.

As long as a man believes he is a creature of external conditions he will be buffeted by those conditions. When he practices self-control and self-purification of thought, and remedies his defects of character, he finds that his circumstances will change.

The soul attracts that which it secretly harbors; its loves and fears. The soul reaches the height of its cherished aspirations and the depth of its desires. Every thought-seed allowed to take root in a man's mind will eventually produce the fruit of character and opportunity and circumstance.

Good thoughts bear good fruit, bad thoughts bad fruit.

EFFECTS OF THOUGHTS ON HEALTH & BODY

The body is the servant of the mind. With unlawful thoughts, the body sinks into disease and decay; with glad and beautiful thoughts it becomes clothed with youthfulness & beauty. Thoughts of fear can kill the body.

Anxiety quickly demoralizes the whole body, opening it to disease, while impure thoughts will shatter the nervous system.

Strong pure and happy thoughts build up the body in vigor and grace.

The habits of thoughts will produce their effects -- good or bad -- upon the body. Thought is the fount of action, life, and manifestation. Make the fountain' pure and all will be pure.

If you would perfect your body, guard your mind. If you would renew your body, beautify your mind. Thoughts of malice, envy, and disappointment, rob the body of its health and grace. A bright, happy, and serene countenance follows from thoughts of joy, goodwill and serenity.

To continually live in thoughts of ill-will, cynicism, suspicion and envy, is to be confined in a self-made prison.

To think well of all, to be cheerful with all, to find the good in all -- such unselfish thoughts are the very portals of heaven.

THOUGHT & PURPOSE

Until thought is linked with purpose there is no intelligent accomplishment. Aimlessness is a vice. They who have no central purpose in their life fall prey to worries, fears, troubles and self-pity, which lead to failure and loss.

A man should conceive of a legitimate purpose in his heart and set out to accomplish it. He should make this purpose the centralizing point of his thoughts.

He should make this purpose his supreme duty and should devote himself to its attainment, not allowing his thoughts to wander into fanciful imaginings. This is the royal road to self-control and true concentration of thought. He may repeatedly fail to accomplish this purpose, but will overcome weaknesses and grow in character -- a measure of true success and the starting point for future power and triumph.

Never Lose Your SWAGGER

Those who are not prepared for the apprehension brought on by having a great purpose should instead fix their thoughts on the faultless performance of their duty, no matter how insignificant it may appear. This discipline will focus their thoughts and develop their resolution.

Strength can be developed by effort and practice, even in the weakest soul. The physically weak can be made strong by patient training and the man of weak thoughts can make them strong by exercising himself in right thinking.

To think with purpose puts one in the ranks of those who know that failure is one of the pathways to success. A man should mentally mark out a straight path to achieving his purpose and rigorously exclude doubts and fears. The will to do springs from the knowledge that we can do.

Doubt and fear are the great enemies of knowledge and must be slain. He who has conquered doubt and fear has conquered failure. Thought allied fearlessly to purpose becomes a creative force.

"THE THOUGHT-FACTOR IN ACHIEVEMENT"

All that a man achieves and all that he fails to achieve is the direct result of his own thoughts. A man's weakness and strength, purity and impurity, are his own and not another man's. They can only be altered by him. His sufferings and his happiness are evolved from within.

As he thinks, so is he; as he continues to think, so he remains.

A strong man cannot help a weaker unless the weaker is willing to be helped. Even then the weak man must become strong of himself -- only he can alter himself.

Oppressor and slaves are cooperators in ignorance and afflict themselves rather than each other. A perfect love condemns neither and a perfect compassion embraces both.

He who has conquered weakness and has pushed away all selfish thoughts belongs neither to oppressor nor oppressed.

He is free.

Never Lose Your SWAGGER

A man can only rise, conquer and achieve by lifting up his thoughts.

Before a man can achieve anything, he must lift his thoughts above animal indulgence. A man whose first thought is bestial indulgence could neither think clearly nor plan methodically. He could not find and develop resources and would fail in any undertaking.

Not having begun to manfully control his thoughts, he is not in a position to control affairs and to adopt serious responsibilities. He is limited by the thoughts he chooses.

A man's worldly success will be by the measure that he sacrifices his confused animal thoughts and fixes his mind on the development of his plans and the strengthening of his resolution and self-reliance. The higher he lifts his thoughts, the greater will be his success.

The universe only appears to favor the greedy, dishonest and vicious. Intellectual achievements are the result of thought consecrated to the search for knowledge or for the beautiful and true in nature.

An intellectual achievement is sometimes connected to vanity and ambition, but is not the outcomes of these.

Spiritual achievements are the consummation of holy aspirations. Achievement of any kind is the crown of effort, the diadem of thought.

By the aid of self-control, resolution, purity, righteousness, and well-directed thought a man ascends. By the aid of animalism, indolence, impurity, corruption and confusion of thought man descends. A man who has risen to high success may descend into great wretchedness by allowing arrogant, selfish and corrupt thoughts to take possession of him.

Victories attained by right thought are maintained by watchfulness. Many give way when success is assured, and rapidly fall back into failure. All achievements -- business, intellectual, and spiritual are the result of definitely directed thought. To achieve greatly one must sacrifice greatly.

Never Lose Your SWAGGER

VISIONS & IDEALS

The dreamers are the saviors of the world. The entire visible world is sustained by the invisible. He who cherishes a beautiful vision, a lofty ideal in his heart, will one day realize it.

To desire is to obtain, to aspire is to achieve.

Shall a man's basest desires receive the fullest measure of gratification, and his purest aspirations starve for lack of sustenance? Dream lofty dreams and as you dream, so shall you become.

Your vision is the promise of what you shall one day be. The greatest achievements were at first and for a time a dream. The Oak sleeps in an acorn.

Dreams are the seedlings of realities.

Uncongenial circumstances can be overcome by perceiving and striving toward and ideal. You cannot travel on the inside and remain still on the outside.

You will always gravitate toward that which you secretly love most. You will become as small as your controlling desire, or as great as your dominant aspiration.

The thoughtless, ignorant and indolent speak of luck, fortune and chance. They do not see the trials, failures and struggles of men who achieve wealth, intellect or holiness. They have no knowledge of the sacrifices, efforts and exercised faith of the latter in overcoming the obstacles to their dreams. They do not know the darkness or the heartaches.

Gifts, powers, material, intellectual and spiritual possessions are the fruits of effort. They are thoughts completed, objectives accomplished, and visions realized. The vision that you glorify in your mind, the ideal that you enthrones in your heart, this you will build your life by; this you will become.

Never Lose Your SWAGGER

SERENITY

Calmness of mind is one of the beautiful jewels of wisdom. It is the result of long and patient effort in self-control. A calm man, having learned how to govern himself, knows how to adapt himself to others. The more tranquil a man becomes, the greater is his success, his influence, his power for good.

The strong, calm, man is always loved and revered.

Only the wise man, only he whose thoughts are controlled and purified, makes the winds and storms of the soul obey him.

To tempest-tossed souls: **Self-control is <u>strength</u>. Right thought is <u>mastery</u>. Calmness is <u>power</u>.** Say unto your heart, "Peace. Be still."

"As a Man Thinketh is written for all those seeking wisdom and tranquility in a turbulent, complex world," suggests its author James Allen.

This clear, concise book has been one of the world's best-selling and most widely loved inspirational works. Allen's words have helped millions for more than a century—and they continue to point the way to a better life for all people.

As a Man Thinketh is birthed by the Bible verse from Proverbs chapter 23 verse 7, "As a man thinketh in his heart, so he is." As Allen expresses it, "Act is the blossom of thought, and joy and suffering are its fruit; thus does a man garner in the sweet and bitter fruitage of his own husbandry."

Allen explains that what a person thinks about is what he or she becomes. He likens the mind to a garden. What is planted will infallibly be grown into the condition of life. The soil does not care whether the seeds are weeds or flowers.

Nature will render whatever is planted. So it is with the mind. Positive thoughts will grow positive results; negative thoughts will spawn negative results:

Allen's words are carefully chosen to speak directly to our innate awareness of our authorship of our own destiny: "He who cherishes a beautiful vision, a lofty ideal in his heart, will one day realize it. Columbus cherished a vision of another world and he discovered it.

Copernicus fostered the vision of a multiplicity of worlds and a wider universe, and he revealed it. Buddha beheld the vision of a spiritual world of stainless beauty and perfect peace, and he entered into it.

THOUGHT CREATES OUR CHARACTER

Author James Allen declares that our character is the product of our thinking: "A noble and Godlike character is not a thing of favor or chance, but is the natural result of continued effort in right thinking, the effect of long-cherished association with Godlike thoughts."

THOUGHT DETERMINES OUR CIRCUMSTANCES

Allen writes, *"Circumstance does not make the man; it reveals him to himself."*

The author concedes "A man cannot directly choose his circumstances," but Allen submits that "he can choose his thoughts, and so indirectly, yet surely, shape his circumstances.

Nature helps every man to the gratification of the thoughts which he most encourages, and opportunities are presented which will most speedily bring to the surface both the good and evil thoughts."

He offers the example of "a rich man who is the victim of a painful and persistent disease as the result of gluttony. He is willing to give large sums of money to get rid of it, but he will not sacrifice his gluttonous desires. He wants to gratify his taste for rich and unnatural foods and have his health as well. Such a man is totally unfit to have health, because he has not yet learned the first principles of a healthy life."

"Cherish your visions; cherish your ideals. Cherish the music that stirs in your heart, the beauty that forms in your mind, the loveliness that drapes your purest thoughts.

Never Lose Your SWAGGER

For out of them will grow all delightful conditions, all heavenly environment; of these, if you but remain true to them, your world will at last be built.

Mind is the master-weaver, both of the inner garment of character and the outer garment of circumstance, and that, as they may have hitherto woven in ignorance and pain they may now weave in enlightenment and happiness."

This book will help you transform your thoughts into concrete actions that will result in the achievement of anything that you deeply desire in your heart:

THOUGHT ESTABLISHES OUR HEALTH

"The body is the servant of the mind," Allen succinctly asserts. "It obeys the operations of the mind, whether they be deliberately chosen or automatically expressed.

At the bidding of unlawful thoughts the body sinks rapidly into disease and decay; at the command of glad and beautiful thoughts it becomes clothed with youthfulness and beauty. Change of diet will not help a man who will not change his thoughts. When a man makes his thoughts pure, he no longer desires impure food."

Purpose is necessary

The author advises, "Until thought is linked with purpose there is no intelligent accomplishment. They who have no central purpose in their life fall an easy prey to worries, fears, troubles, and self-pitying, all of which lead to failure, unhappiness, and loss. Thought allied fearlessly to purpose becomes creative force."

"The dreamers are the saviors of the world."

SWAGGER PURPOSE

*Influence Principles For Attracting and Experiencing
Abundance, Happiness and "Real Purpose In Your Life*

The idea of just how important and powerful having purpose in our lives doesn't really hit us until it is taken from or lost upon us.

As kids, we never really gave it a second thought. By default, purpose was given to us by those around us. Go to school, get good grades, hang out with your friends, watch movies, have fun, rinse and repeat.

Upon graduation from school, that purpose "expired" and a void was left in its place to be filled.

But the problem is that many people don't know what to fill that void with because it's been filled by others around them their entire life so it's no wonder why they have so much difficulty with it in the first place.

Three scenarios come into play at this point in time.

Scenario #1: They attempt to fill that void with something once again, outside themselves. Parents, friends and family give them purpose – do this, do that. Society gives them purpose as well – get a nice comfy job, get rich, get a house in the suburbs, drive nice cars, raise a family, retire.

Never Lose Your SWAGGER

Government gives purpose too – join the army. Be all that you can be. Serve your country.

For the majority of people, having purpose given to them by those around them comes as a major relief as they have something to hold onto now after having their "boat" taken from them in the sea of life.

But the majority of these people will soon realize later on down the road that having purpose handed to them from the outside was like a band aid covering a gaping hole in their chest as they come to the sad conclusion and realize that the purpose their life was built on, did not create the life that they truly wanted deep down inside.

Scenario #2: They go on a journey to find their purpose to fill that void, but soon give up because they cannot find it. At this point, they go back to the first scenario or worse yet, just drift aimlessly through life.

This is probably one of the worst feelings in the world and people suffer through it with quiet desperation. When you're drifting, there's no sense of control, no sense of direction, nothing to shoot for. Life pushes you in every which way and it's hard to get a footing on it.

A feeling of hopelessness and helplessness envelopes you and you begin to wonder if any other people feel the same way. The truth is, a lot of people feel the exact same way, but few will openly acknowledge it out of fear of losing face to those around them.

Rather, they put up a façade that life is great, and just go through the motions, spinning their wheels in the process.

Scenario #3: They realize that the void must be filled, so they go on a journey to find their purpose and never give up until they do, for they know it will be the death of them if they don't. How is life like with purpose?

It is one of the greatest feelings in the world, perhaps best felt the moment one discovers and commits to it.

No longer are you grasping for straws in the mud and being thrown here and there, but now have strong footing and deep roots which enable you to withstand the winds and storms of life. It is such an empowering feeling to have purpose in your life.

You truly feel "alive" in every sense of the word. Your days become much brighter. A radiant glow emanates from your body. Worries seem to become so trivial and a thing of the past. Things become relative as you put them in their proper perspective in accordance to your purpose.

You become satisfied with the decisions you make in your life since you have something that helps correctly guide them in the first place. All your actions and thoughts begin to revolve around your purpose and life as you know it begins to "shape" and "mold" itself according to it.

It is truly one of man's greatest blessings to be able to have the consciousness and ability to choose what their purpose is in life, rather than live the life that animals lead.

It is also indeed a double edged sword, with one side having the potential to unlock within a person, powers that he never knew he had before and the other, potential to forever scatter those same exact powers.

The million dollar question then arises.

What is your purpose?

You know just as well as I do that I cannot give you that answer.

I apologize if that's what you were expecting, but having somebody else tell you what your purpose is counter intuitive to a certain degree. Sure you can give them suggestions as to what their purpose can or should be, but until they acknowledge that the purpose that was suggested is their purpose, in other words, they make it their own, they cannot garner the full benefits from it.

YOU must find your purpose and justify it to yourself because by doing so, you make it your own and once you make it your own, you activate an inner drive within you that's immune to the thoughts and opinions of people outside of you.

Never Lose Your SWAGGER

That nagging feeling of "what will other people think?" goes away. Approval from others doesn't become so important.

If you haven't found your purpose, make it your purpose to find it.

Take the journey. Some say meditate. Some say ask other people who've found their purpose. Some say engage in deep introspection. Take all that. Utilize it. See where it takes you. See where it leads you.

Purpose will be different for many of us simply because we were raised in different circumstances, different cultures, have different beliefs, etc.

But I guarantee you that once you do find your purpose (and you will) an incredible feeling that words cannot describe will wash over you and you'll know in that moment, that you've found it.

I cannot emphasize how important it is that you make sure that your purpose is of your own volition and ONLY your own because once you do that, it can never be taken from you. It becomes something real, something tangible, and something you can hold onto for the rest of your life.

Be ready to justify to yourself that the purpose you have chosen is indeed your own choice and that you consciously made the decision to pursue it. Defend it to yourself. Not to other people, but to yourself, because that is all you need. If you can do that, then that is truly your purpose.

One thing I want to point out is that we can never judge another person for the purpose they choose to follow. Some people may choose money. Some fame. Some charity. Some, a life of solitude. That's fine. That's their purpose and their purpose alone. Not yours.

When you find your purpose and make it your own, it's as if your internal battery gets "jump started" and you really get moving and make traction to take confident steps in harmony with your purpose.

Once you have purpose, you begin to see exactly what you're made of because purpose activates within you your natural success mechanism. Life also helps by giving you all the things you need to help you with your purpose after seeing that you've finally made that decision.

You'll definitely find yourself spending time pursuing it, finding and interacting with people of the same purpose, and encouraging one another to go for it. The people you hang around with, your choice of books and entertainment, your diet, your lifestyle, all of it will start to revolve around your purpose, feeding it and helping you pursue it.

One last thing I want to point out is to make sure that you differentiate between purpose and goals and here is the simple difference between the two:

Goals are there to serve your purpose, not to be your purpose.

Purpose is the driving force behind you setting the goals you want to achieve. Goals are merely a reflection and minor subset of your overall purpose.

Read the lives of men and women who you considered to have lead successful lives from the beginning of history and you will always find, beyond a shadow of a doubt, that having purpose in their lives played a central role in their success.

You'll discover that the one common factor they all had within them is that their purpose was something much something greater than themselves and that they genuinely loved pursuing it.

Whatever your purpose is, when you find it, own it - make it your own, and watch as your life slowly sculpts around it, delivering the necessary resources to aid in your pursuit of it.

In closing, I just want to say that a lot of people may fear, avoid, or even detest the path of finding purpose in their lives because it seems like such an overwhelming task and they fear that they will fail if they undertake it, but by taking on that task and persevering no matter how hard or how long it takes, and going through the journey to find your purpose, that will truly make all the difference, not just in your life, but in the world.

Never Lose Your SWAGGER

YOU must find out what your purpose is. YOU must go on a journey to figure it out because when you undertake the journey to find it (and you eventually will find it), that journey will ready you to successfully pursue it.

THE PURPOSE OF ACCEPTANCE

Discover how the Power Of Acceptance can quite literally transform your life and enable you to begin attracting unlimited Abundance and Happiness into your life.

THE PURPOSE OF ACCEPTING RESPONSIBILITY

Do you believe that you're a "Creature of Circumstance" or a "Creator of Circumstance?"

By becoming aware of WHO is responsible for the current events, conditions, and circumstances in your life you will become empowered to begin the process of attracting abundance and taking focused and intentional action to dramatically transform your results.

THE PURPOSE OF ACTION

Action is without question necessary to accomplish any tangible goal or vision held, but it's not necessarily the type of action that the vast majority has been programmed and conditioned to engage in.

Discover which type of action enables you to tap into your "true power" to begin attracting abundance physically, financially, relationally, emotionally and/or spiritually.

THE PURPOSE OF BEING

The Purpose of Being is the granddaddy of all Purpose and power principles. Overlooking the power behind "consciously initiating" this essential skill and you'll "perceive" yourself as powerless and your life as a random and chaotic unfolding of self-repeating and seemingly inescapable events, conditions and circumstances.

Oh, but you're NOT powerless and life is unfolding perfectly, precisely and for a very specific reason. When you understand the power of being, you'll know that reason.

THE PURPOSE OF BELIEF

A deeper understanding of The Power Of Belief will allow you to discover the true power available to you and your unlimited potential to attract abundance and create a kind and quality of life that the majority only dream about and "wish" they could.

THE PURPOSE OF CHOICE

Are the current choices that you are making in alignment and harmony with attracting and experiencing your desired outcomes? Discover the difference between simply choosing and "consciously choosing."

Whether you may realize it or not, you DO have a choice you know and the understanding difference can transform your life exponentially.

THE PURPOSE OF COMPASSION

When compassion is expressed and utilized consciously and intentionally it has far reaching effects that extend well beyond what most understand. To fully initiate The Power of Compassion in a healthy and wholesome way requires more than expressing compassion to others. Now you'll know how.

THE PURPOSE OF EMOTIONS

The emotions that you experience play a far bigger role in attracting abundance than you may realize in relation to the day to day events, conditions and circumstances that you are currently experiencing. If your life circumstances aren't all that you have a desire for them to be, find out what you can do to change them. You'll be absolutely amazed!

THE PURPOSE OF FOCUS

Your predominant focus is an essential and necessary aspect of attracting abundance and plenty into your life. Where you choose to keep your "attention" determines your often unconsciously held "intention" and will without fail deliver to you precisely what you choose to keep your focus on.

THE PURPOSE OF FORGIVENESS

The Purpose of Forgiveness should never be underestimated and is absolutely essential to enable you to begin attracting Abundance and Happiness into your life.

Find out why.

THE PURPOSE OF GRATITUDE

How it is that Purpose Of Gratitude can affect the life experiences that you encounter from day to day? Being grateful for what you already have opens you up to receive more.

THE PURPOSE OF IMAGINATION

The Purpose of Imagination is said by scientists to be the greatest creative force in the Universe. It can both limit you and enable you to reach heights never before imagined or conceived.

It's simply a matter of learning to consciously utilize it to transcend the self-imposed limitations that you yourself are allowing.

Expand your imagination and you'll expand and enhance your entire life.

THE PURPOSE OF INTENTION

The influence Of Intention without fail provides whatever outcomes you might be experiencing in your life. Become aware and conscious of what you are intending for yourself and you'll have discovered yet another key to experiencing the kind and quality of life that ALL desire yet far too few ever experience.

THE PURPOSE OF LOVE

Love is by far the strongest, most creative and most powerful of all principles. Discover how to harness it's limitless power for profound and pleasing results and the essential role it plays in attracting abundance in every aspect of your life.

THE PURPOSE OF HAVING A MASTERMIND

If you're serious about taking your results in life to the next level, the power of a mastermind group can prove to be a much needed and powerfully effective ally in assisting you in fulfilling your most heartfelt dreams, desires, visions and goals.

Discover for yourself how the power of a mastermind group can assist in attracting abundance and provide enormous benefit.

THE PURPOSE OF MEDITATION

Discover how the Purpose Of Meditation will enable you to tap into never before realized territory and discover the life changing experiences of enlightenment, guidance, heightened awareness, improved health, and profound inner peace.

If you're not doing this you're missing out on FAR more than you know.

THE PURPOSE OF PASSION

Are you fulfilling your heartfelt passion? Find out how discovering and working toward fulfilling what you are passionate about will open doors of opportunity and enable you to experience a sense of harmony and fulfillment that you never previously knew existed.

THE PURPOSE OF PERCEPTION

Do you fully understand the difference between real truth and perceived truth? Your perceptions are merely filters based on beliefs, not all of which are correct. They can certainly make all the difference in how your life experience unfolds. This will show you how and why.

Never Lose Your SWAGGER

THE PURPOSE OF PERSEVERANCE

What does Perseverance have to do with attracting Abundance and Happiness into your life? Whether or not you realize it, it has EVERYTHING to with it.

Discover how and why.

THE PURPOSE OF POSITIVE AFFIRMATIONS

Discover how to "correctly" structure and utilize the Purpose of Positive Affirmations and why they are an essential aspect of attracting abundance and manifesting "desired" results.

THE PURPOSE OF POSITIVE ESTEEM

Do you believe that you are worthy of receiving all that was intended for you? The Power of Positive Self Esteem can make ALL the difference between experiencing mediocre and mind blowing results.

THE PURPOSE OF PRAYER

Many "perceive" that the Power of Prayer is hit and miss at best. Rest assured that it's not and ALWAYS produces an outcome that harmonizes with your choice as "unconscious" as that choosing might be.

Understanding The Power of Prayer and how it never fails or wavers combined with a willingness to master your ability to use it consciously and intentionally will enable and empower you to create miracles in every area of your life.

THE DISCOVERY OF PURPOSE

Discovering and defining your unique and individual purpose for being here will initiate the Power of Purpose in your life and enable you to experience the limitless blessings that are and always have been available to you.

Never Lose Your SWAGGER

THE PURPOSE OF CREATIVE VISUALIZATION

Bringing about the desired results in your life is much simpler than most can imagine and are able to conceive. Discover how the Power of Creative Visualization can assist and empower you to begin consciously and intentionally attracting Abundance and Happiness into EVERY aspect of your life.

THE PURPOSE OF SELF AWARENESS

The Purpose Of Self Awareness goes far beyond who and what you "think" you are or what you are doing from moment to moment in your physical world. Discover what true Self Awareness really is and how it can and does have a dramatic impact in molding and shaping your quality of life.

THE PURPOSE OF SURRENDER

Learn to become detached and ALLOW your life to unfold utilizing The Purpose Of Surrender and you will have discovered the key to a life of fulfillment beyond your wildest expectations. Contrary to widespread belief, attracting abundance isn't about "making" things happen.

THE PURPOSE OF THOUGHT

Did you realize that on average, we as humans think approximately 60,000 thoughts per day? That's A LOT of thinking!! Discover how the power of those thoughts allow you to, or can keep you from, attracting limitless Abundance and Happiness into EVERY aspect of your life.

THE PURPOSE OF TRUST

The Power of Trust may be the last on the list of Success Principles due to placing them in alphabetical order, but don't allow that to keep you from seeing, understanding, believing and trusting that it is perhaps the single most important place to start from to make abundance and happiness a "tangible reality" for you...unconditionally.

Never Lose Your SWAGGER

SWAGGER AWARENESS

We've all heard it: "Get the swagger, get the girls." We can all picture it too.

Guys who are naturally attractive to females just carry themselves differently from the haters on the sidelines. Men with swagger seem more relaxed, more at ease and more ready to laugh; yet, they also seem more alert, more in-tune, and more sure of themselves.

Cultivating swagger is simply a byproduct of two converging forces: **your beliefs** and **your emotional state**.

A man's belief system is probably the greatest or worst investment he will ever make in himself.

Literally, what a man believes will shape every second of his life. No amount of money or success can remedy a set of bad beliefs. Conversely, no amount of depravity or bad luck can shake a man who has positive beliefs. With so much at stake, why would any man choose to wire himself with a bad belief system?

Well, there are lots of reasons.

And most of those reasons are way beyond the scope of a book on swagger so let's only explore the beliefs most relevant to uncovering your swagger.

To get "the swag" you have to stop believing everyone is your friend. Literally, people are either your supportive cheerleaders, or they don't exist at all.

There is **NO** room for haters. If someone wants to spit "Haterade" in your face, that person gets promptly ignored. Any swagger worth its sway repels negativity and attracts awesomeness.

Haters do not apply!

Next, the swag lives by its own standards. A sexy swagger doesn't have time to survey everyone it passes and find out if they all approve. Walking with a swagger is the exact opposite of walking on eggshells.

Men with swagger are men-on-the-move, stomping those eggshells into oblivion. To them, sitting around and wondering whether they're "offending" people is a big waste of time. In fact, an effective swagger must be offensive to some people.

Haters who cannot process the inherent awesomeness of the swag will go into a "hater feeding frenzy" similar to a hungry shark.

Haters lash out at the swagger because they are witnessing the very thing they don't have. So before you put the haters on ignore (per the above paragraph), thank them as they are letting you know that your swagger is so flawless that it's bothering them.

Another belief in the king's crown of swagger is the belief that hooking up with a woman is as much of a win for her as it is for you.

Sounds obvious, yet how many guys drive themselves crazy over making the "perfect" impression?

While there's absolutely nothing wrong with taking pride in everything you do (in fact, that's implicit in having a swagger), there's something very wrong in doing something simply to "impress" another person.

Never Lose Your SWAGGER

That, by definition, is manipulation. If you are a guy who truly believes that a man (with a swagger) and a woman hooking up is a big win for both parties, then you are a guy who saves himself a ton of girl-related headaches by putting women on pedestals like they are somehow better than you just because they're attractive.

With positive beliefs, your swag is halfway there. To get the other half swagging, get the good emotions flowing. While emotions change on a moment-to-moment basis, there are ways to exert some consistency over your emotional health. Just like listening to the Rocky soundtrack will get you amped for the gym, you should know what gets you feeling awesome.

For example, many guys find doing cardio workouts or lifting weights puts them in a positive state.

Also, eating healthy foods like brown carbs (i.e. brown rice, wheat bread), lean protein, and lots of water also helps. Perhaps the quickest and most effective "emotional pump-up" is simply beaming a genuine smile.

It's impossible to simultaneously feel negative and beam a huge smile. Eventually the smile will win and an avalanche of positive feeling and awesomeness will sweep over the body.

It may seem simple, but a true swagger is what separates the Macks from the wannabes. Guys who walk with swagger are constantly trailed by girl-groupies.

If you cement the beliefs and habits above, you will exude attractive confidence with every step you take. Give it a try. Write out (in your own words) the three beliefs and try actively implementing a few of the "emotional pumping" suggestions.

If you're not walking with a swagger within a few weeks, I'll buy you a beer (for real).

Never Lose Your SWAGGER

Prelude

THE RENAISSANCE MAN

E very man should strive to reach his full potential. The competitive world in which we live stresses hyper-specialization as the way to get ahead.

University graduate degrees narrow down a student's area of expertise to enable them fill a specific niche. Young boys are encouraged to choose a single sporting event in which they excel if they are to have any hope for a collegiate or professional career down the road.

Sadly, this trend is slowly eliminating the once-popular aspiration of becoming a well-rounded man.

A gentleman should have a firm handle on not just one or two, but every aspect of his humanity, working to strengthen himself in every way possible.

If he is blessed with the gift of intelligence, his academic pursuits should not be chased to the expense of his physical health. Similarly, a creative personality should not lead a man to isolate himself and ignore the social aspect of his being.

Never Lose Your SWAGGER

Excellence in one of these areas does not take attention away from the pursuit of the others but rather serves only to increase competence in complimentary areas, giving man a greater understanding of himself and the world around him.

The ideal of the Renaissance Man originated in Italy, and is based on the belief that a man's capacity for personal development is without limits; competence in a broad range of abilities and areas of knowledge should be every man's goal and is within every man's grasp.

What follows is a breakdown of the areas you need to master in order to become a true Renaissance Man.

OVERVIEW

During my Life Coaching session for a Men's Ministry retreat someone asked that I give a 12-step plan on being an alpha male.

I suggested some tips on how to stand, talk or dress that would make him more of an alpha male, but I felt unable to fully give him what he was asking for in the detail that he wanted. Why?

First, there are many sites online that already write about such things, and do it much better than I ever could. And the second, and probably more controversial, reason is that I don't really think it's possible for most of us guys to even become alpha males in today's society.

Yes, you read that right.

Too many of the behaviors and attitudes associated with being a true alpha male are either extremely frowned upon socially, or are outright illegal.

The very, very highest level of alpha male throughout history has been the guy who has been willing to either injure or take life (even if by ordering someone under him to do it) or risk injury and even his own death. For example it used to be perfectly acceptable, if a guy insulted you, to punch him in the face if you wanted.

Now in today's society, a guy can pretty much insult you all he wants until the cows come home, but the moment you get sick of it and punch him in the face, you have committed a crime.

Back in the day though, you not only had the option of punching a dude, you could even duel him to the death. I'm sure the number of passive-aggressive people was much lower back then as a result, given repercussions like that.

But not only is it illegal, we have a generation of men socially conditioned to avoid and frown on fighting from the moment they enter the school system.

It's drilled into their heads to the point where the average middle-class guy would do anything to avoid punching another guy in the face, not only because it would be illegal or because he fears the scorn of his community, but also because deep in his heart of hearts he feels like he failed as a civilized human being.

Fighting has become a moral failing in the mind of modern men. The prevalent social attitudes are to either stand there all day and bicker like a woman or take the "high road" and just walk away.

Even guys who have asked me about how to be more alpha in the past, when I suggest punching a guy in the face once in a while when they get fed up as one of the steps, balk at this suggestion. And given the ways the community and the legal system will punish you for engaging physical violence, I can't totally blame them.

I once believed the same thing, but I made a pledge to myself two years ago though that to the best of my ability I would no longer shy away from physical violence to solve problems, or view it as a sign of weakness to do so.

The people who created such rules were women and powerful but physically weak intellectual men who wanted to find a way to level the playing field for themselves against alpha males by using the legal system. Most men are afraid to fight for the same reason they're afraid of approaching women. They're afraid of that ego-shattering sensation of failing, and publicly to boot. It's safer to not try.

With fighting, they even take it one step further by reframing their fear into a virtue, which is why most civilized men will try to portray their unwillingness to fight as a virtue. But that's just one of the many ways society has neutered the ability of men to be alpha males.

Never Lose Your SWAGGER

One of the effects of a society with men totally free to be as alpha as they want is (1) incredible inequality as much of the power and sexual opportunity gets concentrated in the hands of the few and powerful, and (2) lack of security for the average person.

Societies with unbridled alpha aggression free a man to go for the things he wants, but also leave him open to someone bigger and stronger doing the same thing to him at some point. And for women, these societies can be especially dangerous and volatile.

As societies become more civilized and become more democratic, they tend to start valuing things like equality and security above all else. Consequently these civilized societies start relegating all alpha status to the state, and to its enforcement arm, the legal system, in exchange for more equality and security. The State is the biggest alpha in America now.

The only individuals who can achieve true alpha status in the West nowadays are the people who are rich and powerful enough to influence and control the state.

They refuse to play by the State's rules and thumb their nose at its legal system enforcement arm, and the members that make up the frontline of that aforementioned enforcement arm such as police, prosecutors and military men in times of war. The only option available for the rest of us is to be as much of a man as we can while still toeing the line acceptable in today's society.

We can only be Alpha within limits. So in trying to come up with a term beside Alpha Male, I decided to use Renaissance Man instead. This is a term that is also used by Tariq Nasheed. The Renaissance Man is a modern man who is as alpha as he can be despite not being rich and powerful and while still living within the limitations set upon him by society and his power level.

You can often see examples of such men in old movies that were made before the 70s.

CREDITS & ACKNOWLEDGMENTS

A large amount of inquiries were conducted during the process of composing **Never Lose Your Swagger**.

The Swagger Concepts and Labels are an extension of the Coaching Series that has been widely researched and supported by the various references mentioned herein.

Akami University Men's Studies Program is designed to investigate, in a gender-specific manner, the many forces and issues affecting men in today's society.

The mission of the program is to prepare and empower graduates to make far-reaching contributions in a variety of professional settings.

The American Men's Studies Association is a not for profit professional organization of scholars, therapists, and others interested in the exploration of masculinity in modern society. As the members and supporters of the Men's Studies movement forward their suggestions, they will be considered for incorporation in this page.

Bentley Coaching Institute with Dr. J'Ramando Horton Provides five levels of certification in various life coaching specialty areas. The Bentley Leadership University is an international training and consulting company specializing in the "soft-skills" side of business.

Our instructors and trainers are experts in developing strong, confident leaders throughout many companies and independent businesses both locally and internationally as well purposefully shifting and creating fun, high energy corporate cultures for clients.

Men's Programs, Pierce College
Helping men succeed in higher education.

The Changing Men Collection, Michigan State University This includes materials devoted to father's rights, the National Organization of Men Against Sexism, mytho-poetic groups, and groups representing men's issues from all over the world. The CMC also features a large collection of periodicals and newsletters.

Culture in the Schools with Joe Manthey

Offering three programs: Kid Culture in the Schools for educators, Raising Good Sons for parents, and How Boys Are Shortchanged in the Schools for high school students.

Embracing Your Father: Strengthening Father-Daughter Relationships

Providing daughters, fathers, practitioners, and professors with ideas and resources for strengthening father-daughter relationships. Specific, no-nonsense advice while introducing people to the best available research and statistics on father-daughter relationships.

Family Violence Laboratory

Since 1975, the Family Research Laboratory (FRL) has devoted itself primarily to understanding family violence and the impact of violence in families. As public and professional interest in family violence has grown, so has the need for more reliable knowledge.

The FRL has tried to fill that need in a variety of ways: through comprehensive literature reviews, new theories, and methodologically sound studies.

The Journal of Men's Studies seeks to publish the best scholarship in the emerging field of Men' Studies recognizing the varied influences of class, culture, race, and sexual orientation on defining men's experiences. JMS's cross-disciplinary and cross-cultural character disseminates material by men's studies scholars from various perspectives (political, social, cultural, historical), as well as various disciplines (anthropology, sociology, history, psychology, literature, religious studies).

Topics of interest include but are not limited to issues involving men's relations with others, the continual tensions between the competing and contradictory roles men play in their ever-changing world, and the social construction of masculinities.

The Men's Bibliography

A comprehensive bibliography of writing on men, masculinities and sexualities (6th edition)

Never Lose Your SWAGGER

Contact: Michael Flood, PO Box 26, Ainslie, Canberra, ACT 2602
AUSTRALIA

Men Teach

MenTeach, a national nonprofit organization, was founded in 1979 as
Men in Child Care & Elementary Education Project. It serves as a
clearinghouse for research, education and advocacy with a commitment
to increase the number of men teaching young children in early and
elementary education.

Psychology of Men and Masculinity

This quarterly journal is devoted to the dissemination of research,
theory, and clinical scholarship that advances the discipline of the
psychology of men and masculinity. This discipline is defined broadly
as the study of how men's psychology is influenced and shaped by
gender, and by the process of masculinization, in both its socially
constructed and biological forms.

Editor: David Lisak, PhD

The Society for the Psychological Study of Men and Masculinity
(Division 51)

The Society for the Psychological Study of Men and Masculinity

(SPSMM) is a Division of the American Psychological Association
(APA). Founded at the 1990 APA convention in Boston (initially as a
separate organization), the Society became a candidate division of APA
in 1995 and a permanent division in 1997.

The Society consists of men and women dedicated to promoting the
critical study of how gender shapes and constricts men's lives and
committed to the enhancement of men's capacity to experience their
full human potential.

Personal Development Planet
Personal-Development-Planet.com

www.ingramcontent.com/pod-product-compliance
Lightning Source LLC
Chambersburg PA
CBHW071805090426
42737CB00012B/1960